Collins

a year of nature craft and play

52 things to make and do

Becky Goddard-Hill & Catherine Hughes

Published by Collins
An imprint of HarperCollins*Publishers*
Westerhill Road, Bishopbriggs, Glasgow G64 2QT
www.harpercollins.co.uk

HarperCollins*Publishers*
1st Floor, Watermarque Building,
Ringsend Road, Dublin 4, Ireland

A catalogue record for this book is available from the British Library

ISBN 978-0-00-846794-4

10 9 8 7 6 5 4 3 2 1

Printed in Bosnia and Herzegovina by GPS Group

If you would like to comment on any aspect of this book, please contact us at the above address or online.

MIX
Paper from
responsible sources
FSC™ C007454

FSC
www.fsc.org

This book is produced from independently certified
FSC™ paper to ensure responsible forest management.

For more information visit: www.harpercollins.co.uk/green

Huge thanks to Michelle I'Anson, Lauren Murray, Hilary Stein, Kevin Robbins and Gordon MacGilp for the vision and creativity to bring this nature book to life.

In loving memory of my gorgeous granddad Arthur Williamson and his beautiful rose-filled garden. He taught me to be creative, resourceful and nurturing. He was my inspiration and bestest friend.

Becky

Thanks to my nature adventure buddies, Sam and Lily, whose enthusiasm and imagination made this book such a joy to create.

Catherine

Author of *Create Your Own Happy*, *Create Your Own Calm*, and *Create Your Own Kindness*, Becky Goddard-Hill is a children's therapist and former social worker with a specialism in child development. She is also a professionally qualified life coach and member of the National Council of Psychotherapists. She is an enthusiastic believer in the power of creativity and nature to support children's emotional health and wellbeing.

Catherine Hughes has turned a lifelong passion for nature and gardening into a thriving career as a home and garden writer and blogger. Catherine's blog *Growing Family* has been a Vuelio Top 10 gardening blog for the last four years. She is passionate about encouraging children to explore and enjoy nature, and writes regularly on crafts, children's gardening and nature activities.

Contents

Autumn

Winter

Index

Introduction

Hello and welcome to this activity-packed book of nature craft and play ideas.

Nature is the best and most brilliant craft and play resource because it is interesting, amazing, inspiring, free, readily available and on your doorstep.

As well as craft and play ideas, there are gardening projects, events, science experiments, and art activities for you to try – and you don't even have to wait for a sunny day.

These activities can be done throughout the year, using things you can easily find in nature. You can do one every week, or dip in and out whenever you feel like it.

You are part of an absolutely amazing natural world. Spending time exploring, enjoying and crafting with nature will help you connect with it – and the more connected you feel, the more you will want to look after it. Nature really does need your help, and hopefully the activities in this book inspire you to take care of and protect our wonderful world.

The countryside code – guidance on how we need to behave in the countryside – is important, and we would ask you to make sure that you follow it when you're enjoying the activities in this book.

Here's what the countryside code asks us to do:

Respect everyone
- Be considerate to those living in, working in and enjoying the countryside.

- Leave gates and property as you find them.

- Do not block access to gateways or driveways when parking.

- Be nice, say hello, share the space.

- Follow local signs and keep to marked paths unless wider access is available.

Protect the environment
- Take your litter home – leave no trace of your visit.

- Do not light fires and only have BBQs where signs say you can.

- Always keep dogs under control and in sight.

- Bag and bin dog poo – any public waste bin will do.

- Care for nature – do not cause damage or disturbance, and only pick fallen flowers or flowers from your own garden or with permission.

Enjoy the outdoors
- Check your route and local conditions.

- Plan your adventure – know what to expect and what you can do.

- Enjoy your visit, have fun, make a memory.

Pass it on
We would love it if you could help us spread the word about how amazing and fun nature can be.

If you try an activity in the book and enjoy it, please pass it on to a friend who you think might enjoy it too.

If you make something beautiful from nature and think it might make someone smile, please pass it on.

And if you complete all the activities in this book, rather than leave it on a shelf, please pass it on!

Wishing you happy and creative nature-filled days.

Love Becky & Catherine

Craft tips

Using natural materials like leaves, flowers, sticks and stones to craft with is always fun and there are endless possibilities to the things you can make.

When you craft from nature the materials you use are naturally produced and recyclable, so it is much better for the environment.

Because your materials are natural rather than manmade, they will have a shorter life cycle. Leaves will crumble, feathers will shrivel and flowers will wilt. This is just part of life. Rather than feel sad your craft won't last forever, think instead how lovely it is that what you have created hasn't harmed the planet in any way.

Here are some crafts tips to help you preserve your leaves and feathers as long as possible and some ideas for helping your crafts last longer. We also have some lovely ideas for gifts you can make from nature too.

Happy nature crafting!

Preserving leaves

Leaves are really exciting to use in nature crafts, but they quickly go dry and crumbly.

One of the easiest ways to preserve leaves is to cover them with Mod Podge™. You can get Mod Podge™ from any craft store, or you can make it yourself. Simply add 1 cup of normal PVA glue to 1/3 cup of water and give it a good stir. It dries clear, so it's a fabulous way to protect a leaf without spoiling how it looks.

You will need

- Greaseproof or baking paper
- Some Mod Podge™
- Leaves in a variety of colours
- A paintbrush

How to preserve leaves

1. Lay the leaves out separately on a piece of greaseproof or baking paper.

2. Paint them with a thin layer of Mod Podge™. Do this gently so as not to tear them.

3. Once they are dry, turn them over and paint the other side, then leave to dry completely. They will be lovely and shiny, and should be good to use in your crafts for at least a month or more.

Did you know?

Do you know why leaves change colour in autumn? Well they don't, not really. They have the other colours there all along but the green (chlorophyll) overpowers them in the summer. Chlorophyll helps make food for the tree and helps leaf stems stay strong.

With less light in the autumn, chlorophyll fades. This makes the leaf stems weaker, which is why the leaves fall off and stop looking green!

Preparing feathers

Feathers are great for crafting. You can use them to make headbands or dreamcatchers, you can dip them in ink and write with them, or try to identify birds with them.

Because feathers have fallen to the ground, they will be dirty and will definitely need a clean before you use them.

It's best to wear gloves when you pick them up. If you're not wearing gloves, then avoid putting your hands near your mouth after touching them.

Give your hands a good soapy clean after gathering feathers.

You will need

- Warm soapy water (containing a little squirt of washing-up liquid)
- A bowl or jug
- Paper towels

How to clean feathers

1. Shake off any loose dirt or bugs.

2. Place your feathers into the water, with the barbs pointing downwards. Make sure they don't get tangled up with each other.

3. Gently swish each one around in the water, being careful not to break them.

4. Rinse by swirling them gently in clean water.

5. Reshape the feather with your fingers.

6. Leave them to dry on a paper towel.

Did you know?

Birds give their feathers special oils that make them waterproof, but once the feathers fall off the bird the oils fade away. This makes the feathers fragile in water, which is why you have to handle them so carefully.

Craft gifts

Have you ever made your own gifts instead of buying them?

A home-made gift is a lovely way to give someone a truly personal present. They are fun to make, they don't cost lots of money, and we can use nature to inspire us and provide our materials.

Christmas is an obvious time for making home-made gifts, but you can of course give them at other times of the year for things like birthdays, Valentine's Day, Mother's Day and Father's Day.

Ideas for craft gifts

- Press some flowers and use them to make cards or bookmarks.

- Create a piece of artwork using natural materials – you could make a collage of nature treasures or try some printing.

- Make a posy of fallen wildflowers.

- Make a leaf wreath.

- Make yarn sticks by wrapping wool around sticks to look like forever flowers.

- Plant a pot with flowering plants or bulbs.

- Make a leaf lantern by gluing dried leaves around a jar and adding an electric tealight.

- Paint a stone to create a unique paperweight.

- Bake some biscuits with natural flavouring such as lavender or mint.

- Make a simple wind chime using shells and string.

Perhaps you could head out for a walk in nature, and see what inspires you? You could make something totally unique.

Preserving crafts

Nature crafts only last until the leaf blows away or the berry shrivels, but that's not a bad thing. Nature crafts don't clutter our homes or put any stress on the environment. They just go back to where they came from and end up as compost, or food for the animals.

Sometimes though, you may really want to keep that amazing craft you worked so hard to create.

A photo album or display
You can keep your nature crafts forever if you photograph them and even create a photo album of your craft projects so you can look at them again. Mini pegs and string are a lovely way to show off your nature craft photos.

Scrapbook
Scrapbooks are great fun to put together and are a lovely way to keep your nature craft memories.

If you were making a nature craft scrapbook, you might add leaves or recipes, or perhaps some found feathers. You might add photos of your crafts, a scavenger hunt list, or a map of where you have been.

Memory making
You don't need to keep something physically in order to remember it. Telling someone about something you made plants it even deeper into your memory. Do talk about your creations; telling your family and friends what you have made might even inspire them to have a go themselves.

Spring

Spring is such an exciting time of year in nature.

The warmer weather and longer days mean lots of plants and trees are waking up and growing fast, giving us a wonderful display of beautiful fresh leaves and flowers. We can join in the celebration by planting seeds, growing our own food and exploring natural wonders whenever we're outdoors.

Wildlife is busy in spring too. Lots of creatures are working hard to look after their babies, re-stock food supplies and build shelters. Making our gardens more wildlife-friendly will help take care of them.

Spring also gives us the chance to have lots of fun outdoors, using nature as our inspiration for crafts, games and exploring.

Step outside, and let spring put a smile on your face.

1 | A sensory spring scavenger hunt

Spring is all about the world waking up again after winter, so it's the perfect time to have a scavenger hunt to wake up all of your senses too. You won't be able to tick off all of these on just one walk, so if it takes all spring to complete the list, that's absolutely fine!

Try and be super-aware with all your senses of the signs of spring around you.

How many of these amazing spring experiences can you touch, taste, hear, smell or see?

Touch / Feel

A smooth pebble ☐   A gentle breeze ☐   The bark of a tree ☐

The sun shining on your face ☐   A fluffy feather ☐   Your feet splashing in a puddle ☐

Taste

The rain on your tongue ☐

A herb (like mint or parsley) ☐

Hear

Birds singing in the morning ☐

Frogs ribbeting ☐

A cat mewing ☐

Ducks quacking ☐

Lambs bleating ☐

Water bubbling ☐

Smell

A flower

Freshly mown grass

Blossom

Moss

Laundry on the washing line

See

Dew on the grass

Yellow daffodils

Green buds on a tree

A butterfly

A rainbow

A bird's nest

A baby animal

2 | Be a soil detective

Soil is made up of lots of different ingredients. These include sand, clay, silt (which is really fine sand or clay), little stones, and plant material such as leaves.

The amount of each ingredient will affect the type of soil you end up with: sandy soil, clay soil, or silt soil.

If you want to grow healthy plants in your garden, it's important to know what type of soil you have, because some plants love growing in a particular type of soil.

This simple experiment will help you work out your soil type, so you can grow plants that will be happy in it.

You will need

- A jam jar with clear, straight sides and a lid

- A sample of soil from your garden

- Water

- A ruler

> *We are part of the earth and it is part of us.*
> Chief Seattle

How to be a soil detective

1. Wash and dry your jam jar.

2. Fill it to about one third full with soil.

3. Pour water into the jar until it is nearly full.

4. Screw the lid onto the jar, then shake it for about five minutes until everything is nicely mixed together.

5. Leave your jar on a flat surface for about a day. Don't move it during this time.

6. Take a look at your jar – has the mixture separated into different layers?

The heaviest ingredients will have sunk to the bottom of the jar and will form a layer. You might see a layer of stones or sand. Silt is the next heaviest ingredient, so there will be a layer of this on top of the sand, followed by clay. The water will sit on top of these – it will probably look dirty. Right at the top you'll see the lightest ingredient, the plant material.

7. Measure the total height of the mixture, then measure the height of each individual layer.

8. Work out the percentage of each layer using this sum:

Height of layer ÷ height of total mixture x 100.

9. The best soil should be about 40% sand, 40% silt and 20% clay.

If your sample has more sand, your soil will drain easily and you can grow plants that don't like sitting in lots of water.

If it has more clay or silt, it will hold onto water and be better for plants that like growing in damp soil.

Great detecting!
Why don't you try soil from a different place and see if it measures the same?

3 | Make a mini pond

Adding a pond to your garden is a brilliant way to encourage more wildlife to visit. It can be as small as a washing-up bowl and still provide a home and food for all sorts of creatures. You don't even need a garden – you could put your pond on a balcony, or outside your front door.

You will need

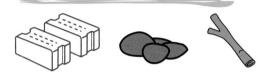

- A watertight container such as a washing-up bowl or bucket

- Large stones or bricks

- Small stones or gravel

- Two or three aquatic plants

- A piece of wood or plastic to make a ramp

- Some sticks

How to make a mini pond

1. Before you put anything into your container, decide where your pond is going to go. It should be somewhere that gets plenty of light, but isn't in full sunlight all day.

2. Put your large stones or bricks in the bottom of your container, then add your smaller stones or gravel on top. Try to make a range of different depths across it.

3. Use some of the stones and bricks to make a slope up to the edge of the container in one place, so that creatures can get in and out easily.

4. Fill your pond with water. Rainwater is better than tap water because it doesn't contain as many chemicals.

5. Add your pond plants. They will be happiest if you put them in aquatic plant pots first, which you can get from the same place you buy your plants. You might need to add some gravel to the pots to weigh them down.

Here are some great options for mini pond plants:
- Rigid hornwort, water starwort and whorled water-milfoil will sit under the water and help to keep it clear.

- Lesser spearwort, marsh marigold and flowering rush will be happy planted around the edge and sticking out of the water.

- A miniature waterlily will float on top of the water.

6. Use a stick to create a bridge on the top of your pond, with one end sticking out over the edge. Add your ramp up the side of your pond, so that creatures can get in and out from the ground.

7. Leave your pond alone and the wildlife will soon move in.

Tips and ideas
You can have fun observing all the wildlife that visits your pond. You could keep a creature diary, draw pictures, or make a bar chart from your study.

Once your pond has lots of residents, you can have a go at pond dipping and investigate the creatures in more detail with a magnifying glass.

Keep safe
Wash your hands when you've finished making your pond.

Small children should always be supervised when playing near your mini pond.

When we show our respect for other living things, they respond with respect for us.
Arapaho proverb

23

4 | Easter activities

Easter games and crafts have been done for hundreds of years and are still great fun to do today. Here are a few of our favourites.

Egg rolling

Egg rolling, or 'pace-egging' as it is sometimes known, is a centuries-old Easter tradition.

All you have to do is boil the eggs for 10 minutes in their shells so they don't break, decorate them in bright colours so they can be seen easily, and then gather friends and family to have a competition to see whose egg can roll the furthest down a nearby grassy hill.

Egg and spoon

Egg and spoon races are also great fun. You simply need enough hard-boiled and decorated eggs for everyone wanting to take part, some spoons large enough to hold the eggs, and a start and finish line. The first person to cross the finish line with their egg still on their spoon is the winner. You could make it more exciting by hopping on one leg instead of running, turning round three times before you start, doing it as a three-legged race, or using the hand you don't write with!

An alternative egg hunt

If you have an egg allergy, are vegan or just don't have any eggs, then how about devising a little treasure hunt? You can make a couple of Easter-themed swag bags for participants and hide painted egg-shaped stones round your garden for them to find.

To make your Easter swag bags, simply draw a bunny outline on a paper bag in black pen and fill in its ears with flowers and leaves to make it look like an Easter bunny.

To paint your stones, choose a smooth stone and use pens that mark on stones. You will need to paint over with varnish or a sealant to stop the colours washing away.

Decorating eggs with nature

You will need

- Hard-boiled eggs in their shells.

- Bits of nature (sticks, fallen flowers, leaves). Flowers and leaves need to be flattened, so ideally use some you have already pressed OR just pop them between paper and place in the middle of a heavy book with other books on top for a few hours.

- Mod Podge™ and glue (see page 10).

How to make....
Use a paintbrush to spread Mod Podge™ onto the egg. Press the flowers and leaves into it to make any pattern you like then Mod Podge™ again lightly over the top to seal it. Whiskers and ears made of sticks can be glued on with ordinary glue.

Happy Easter!

5 | Make a nature loom

Making a nature loom is a fun craft to do on your own or with (lots of) other people. Before you can make your nature loom, you need to go on a nature walk to collect a host of (fallen) colourful treasures such as leaves, feathers, seed pods, grasses, flowers and weeds.

You will need

• Four sticks to make the frame. These all need to be the same length, but can be whatever size and thickness you want.

• Some twine or string to tie the corners of the frame together

• Wool or string to make the inside of the loom

How to make your nature loom

1. Lay out your sticks to make a square, then tightly tie the two sticks together at each corner to make a frame.

2. Tie a piece of string or wool to the bottom of the frame near the edge, and run it up to the stick at the top.

3. Loop your string twice around the top stick, then run it back down to the bottom stick and wrap it twice around that. Repeat.

4. Keep the strings about 1 cm apart across the frame, and keep them pulled tight.

5. Tie the string off tightly when you get to the end of the frame.

6. Next, simply weave your treasures through the strings of the loom, going under and over each string as you thread the items on. You can add them at random or in a pattern.

Display your nature loom in a window or in your garden and it will look amazing.

You can use it again and again by simply removing the items you have woven in and replacing them with something new.

You could use your loom every season if you wanted!

Think bigger!
If you enjoyed making your nature loom you could consider making a giant one in your park for your community to decorate or perhaps doing it as a class project at school.

6 | Make a bee hotel

Bees do a really important job of pollinating food crops, which means they help to provide about a third of all the food we eat. Isn't that amazing?

But bees are struggling to survive because of climate change, chemicals used in farming and more of the countryside being built on.

The good news is that you can help bees by making your garden more bee-friendly. Lots of types of bees love to make their homes in little holes, so one easy way to help them is to make a bee hotel.

You will need

- A terracotta plant pot or empty, clean plastic bottle

- Some sandpaper

- Modelling clay or air-drying clay

- Bamboo canes

- Scissors or secateurs

- Some string

- Stickers or colourful sticky tape (optional)

How to make a bee hotel

1. If you're using a terracotta plant pot, clean out any soil and dirt first.

2. If you're using a plastic bottle, ask a grown-up to cut the top off and sand the edge to make sure it isn't sharp.

3. Put some clay in your container.

4. Ask a grown-up to help you cut up the garden canes so they fit into your container. To work out how long the pieces need to be, stand a cane in the container and cut it off where it meets the top. Cut the rest of the cane into pieces the same size.

> **Question:** Why do bees have sticky hair?
> **Answer:** Because they use honey combs!

5. Fill your container with the pieces of cane, pushing them into the clay to hold them steady. Pack them in as tightly as you can.

6. If you'd like to, you can decorate your bee hotel with stickers or colourful tape.

7. If your bee hotel is made from a plastic bottle, tie two lengths of string around it and use them to hang it up.

8. If it's a terracotta pot, place it on its side on the ground. Choose a quiet spot.

9. Keep an eye on your bee hotel to see who moves in. Solitary bees will make their home in the hollow canes. If a hole is blocked up with leaves that means you have a guest!

Tips and ideas

To make your garden even more bee-friendly, you could add plants that are loved by pollinating insects, grow some wildflowers, or leave dead plant stems or branches out to provide shelter.

Bees work very hard, and sometimes you might see an exhausted bee on the ground. Come to its rescue by making a sugar solution from sugar and warm water, then putting it in a small saucer, bottle cap or spoon, and carefully placing it near the bee's head. The high-energy drink will soon perk it up so it can fly away.

Keep safe

It's lovely to watch bees in your garden, but don't try to touch them or pick them up. Bees aren't aggressive, but they might feel scared and try to sting you.

7 Sensational Sunflowers

Sunflowers are fantastic plants to grow from seed. You can grow them in pots or in the ground, their flowers are seriously impressive, and your local wildlife will love them too.

Sunflowers get their name from their behaviour. The flowers follow the movement of the sun. They like sunbathing!

Plant sunflower seeds in spring, and you will have beautiful flowers in summer.

You will need

- A packet of sunflower seeds
- Some small plant pots
- Some compost
- A trowel
- Gardening gloves
- Plant labels
- A pen or pencil

How to grow sunflowers

1. Use your trowel to fill your plant pot with compost until it's almost full.

2. Use your finger to poke a hole in the middle of the compost.

3. Drop a seed into the hole.

4. Add more compost to fill up the hole.

5. Write a plant label and stick it in your pot.

6. Water your pot until the soil is damp.

7. Put your pot in a warm, bright place. A sunny windowsill is perfect. Check it regularly, and water if the soil feels dry.

8. Your sunflower seed should start to grow within 1–2 weeks.

9. When your sunflower plant has grown bigger, you can transfer it to a bigger pot or plant it in your garden.

10. You also need to give your sunflower plant support to help it grow tall and strong. Push a garden cane into the soil next to the stem, and use string to tie the stem to the cane.

> "Turn your face to the sun, and the shadows fall behind you.
> Maori proverb

Tips and ideas

Why not have a sunflower-growing competition with your family, friends or neighbours? Everyone plants their own sunflower seed and cares for it as it grows. The winner is the person whose plant grows the tallest. Remember to put your name on your pots so you know whose they are.

Birds love sunflower seeds, so when your sunflower heads turn brown, leave them in the garden for the birds to enjoy.

Keep safe

Always wear gloves when you're gardening, and wash your hands when you've finished.

Don't ever eat sunflower seeds that are designed to be planted.

8 | Earth Day

Earth Day began in 1970 in the USA and is celebrated on 22 April each year.

It is a day to think about our planet and what we can do to keep it healthy.

More than a billion people in 192 countries take part in celebrating Earth Day, and you could join in too.

Here are some ideas to help you celebrate our planet:

1. Meet other families for a picnic in the park and combine it with a litter pick.

2. Host a book swap with your friends or pile your old ones onto a table for passers-by to take.

3. Craft something cool from items in your recycling bin.

4. Have a car-free weekend. You could walk, cycle, scoot or skateboard everywhere!

5. Sort through your toys or clothes and fill up a bag for the charity shop.

6. Turn off your technology and spend the day reading, playing, baking and getting out and about.

7. Donate your pocket money to an environmental cause.

8. Get up super early to see the sunrise.

9. Plant an apple seed in a little pot.

10. Have a shower instead of a bath (or do without completely!).

11. Camp out in your garden.

12. Make an Earth Day poster for your window.

13. Have a barefoot disco on the grass.

14. Hug a tree!

15. Upcycle something to use as a planter.

Perhaps you could come up with some Earth-loving ideas of your own!

If Earth Day falls on a school day, you could encourage your teacher to let you have a class party that involves planting runner beans, making bird feeders or having your lessons outside? Or you could have a nature treasure hunt, watch a nature documentary or make a huge display about ways to be kinder to our Earth.

> Be part of the solution, not the pollution.
> Unknown

It'll be lots of fun coming up with class ideas and even more fun putting them into action.

Last year for Earth Day we made up some wildflower seed packets to give away to passers-by.

We have a beautiful world that needs us to appreciate and protect it, every day of the year.

Make every day Earth Day.

9 | Make a miniature garden

Making a miniature garden is something you can do again and again and it can be completely different every time.

If you want to make one that lives outside, you'll need to make sure the items you include are pretty weatherproof. But apart from that, anything goes and you can be as creative as you like!

You might want it to be a home for the fairies, somewhere for your LEGO™ mini figures to hang out, or just a pretty addition to your garden or balcony.

Always start projects like these with a plan, then gather what you need before making a start, but there are no rules when you are being creative.

You will need

• A container for your garden – ideas could include a tinfoil tray, a Tupperware™ box, a planter, a plant pot, a hanging basket, an old bowl, a big teacup or a bucket

• Some moss, flowers, stones, pebbles, twigs, sticks, leaves, soil, shingle and possibly some herbs or tiny plants

• Some fabric, string and glue

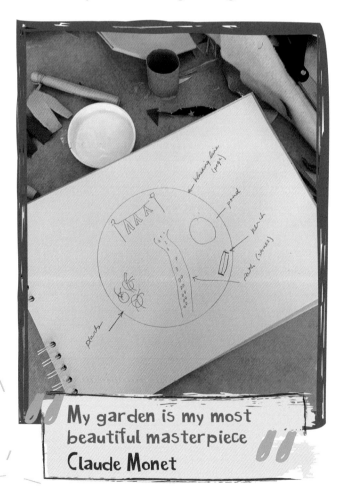

My garden is my most beautiful masterpiece
Claude Monet

How to make your miniature garden

1. Draw a rough sketch of how you want your garden to look.

2. Add a layer of soil to your container to create a base that you can arrange your stones onto and plant your mini plants into.

3. Next, build your pathways and any solid buildings.

4. Leave anything that's delicate till last, so it doesn't get covered in soil or knocked with the stones.

5. It's fun to include a star of the show or a main feature to your miniature garden. For example, the colourful washing line, which was made by tying string across two twigs and cutting up old bits of fabric.

6. Once it's complete, give your garden a little water spray so it isn't all dry and crumbly. You might want to sprinkle some wildflower seeds on it too so it keeps on growing.

7. If it is going to live outside, do try to place it somewhere a bit sheltered so it's protected from the weather. Tend to it now and again, replacing things or removing things that have died, and giving it a little water.

If you want to make a mini garden that can live indoors, you can use any kind of materials and a mixture of natural finds and crafty bits and bobs. Raid the recycling bin for things to use in your crafts.

An indoor miniature garden makes a lovely gift for an older relative who may not get out much.

10 | Grow microgreens

Microgreens are seedlings of herbs and vegetables that you harvest and eat while they are still tiny. They are packed with nutrients and flavour, which means they're good for you and also super-tasty.

Microgreens grow really quickly, and you can usually harvest them about two weeks after you plant the seeds. You don't even need a garden, just a windowsill.

You will need

- A packet of microgreen seeds

- Plant pots, foil trays or recycled takeaway containers

- Some compost

- A small watering can or spray bottle

How to grow microgreens

1. If you're using a recycled container to grow your microgreens, make sure it is clean before you start.

2. Add compost to your container until it's almost full.

3. Scatter your seeds over the top of the compost, as evenly as you can.

4. Sprinkle a little bit more compost on top to cover the seeds.

5. If your container has drainage holes, put it on a saucer or tray.

6. Water your container. The easiest way to do this is to use a spray bottle, but you can also use a small watering can or jug. Try not to soak the soil too much.

7. Put your container in a warm, bright place indoors. A sunny windowsill is perfect.

8. Check your seeds every day, and water them if the soil feels dry. You might also need to turn the container round to stop the seedlings leaning towards the light.

9. When your seedlings are about 5 cm tall, they're ready to harvest. Use scissors to snip them off just above the soil.

10. Eat your microgreens! They're brilliant in salads, sandwiches and smoothies.

Tips and ideas

Carry out a taste test with your microgreens. Does each variety taste like the fully-grown herb or vegetable? If you grew a mixed pack of seeds, can you guess which is which?

Microgreens are sometimes described as 'vegetable confetti' because they add lots of colour to a meal. Can you think of a meal that you'd like to use them on, then ask a grown-up to help you cook it?

Keep safe
Wash your hands when you've finished planting your seeds.

11 | Upcycling

Did you know that millions of plastic plant pots end up in landfill each year?

One great way of avoiding adding to this problem is to get upcycling and use things you already have as planters! Here are a couple of ideas you might like to try.

You will need

- An old container
- Spray paint (optional)
- Some stones or lining material, depending on the container
- Some compost
- Seeds, bulbs, herbs or bedding plants

> There is no such thing as 'away'. When we throw anything away it must go somewhere.
>
> Annie Leonard

Welly pots

It is easy to make plant pots out of your old wellies.

1. Wash your wellies using warm soapy water, so they look fabulous. Remove the bottom liner from the inside.

2. Ask a grown-up to drill or hammer some holes through each sole for the water to drain out.

3. Fill the bottom with stones to stop your welly blowing away!

4. Add in some compost, pressing down firmly up to about 5 cm from the top of each welly.

5. Now add your bulbs or seeds or little plants and fill up with more compost.

Colander planter

A colander is perfect because it already has the holes for the water to drain away.

1. Give the colander a good wash and dry.

2. If you want to change its colour, carefully spray paint it (with adult supervision). Then leave it to dry.

3. Line the inside of the colander with coffee filters or cut a circle out of a piece of burlap fabric to help hold the soil in the colander. If you don't have these, place a layer of stones, pebbles or gravel at the bottom and slightly up the sides before you add your soil.

4. Fill it with soil up to 5 cm from the top, then add any plants, seeds or herbs you like. Fill it to the top with soil and water it.

5. You can hang your planter with string or leave it free-standing.

6. Good plants for a hanging basket include petunias, pansies and lobelia. These spread well and don't need a lot of care.

You could also use old teapots and teacups, old toys, old tyres, tin cans, biscuit barrels, and pretty much any container you can think of! Just make sure that there are little holes for the water to drain out, and your imagination is your only limit!

12 Hapa Zome

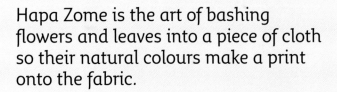

Hapa Zome is the art of bashing flowers and leaves into a piece of cloth so their natural colours make a print onto the fabric.

It was created by an eco-artist called India Flint when she was working in Japan. Hapa Zome in Japanese means 'leaf dye'.

It is a simple, natural way to dye fabric and is lots of fun!

You will need

- Two pieces of cotton fabric (such as an old pillowcase, hanky, or piece of muslin – white works best)

- Some fresh flowers

- Some colourful leaves

- A chopping board

- A rolling pin, rubber mallet or large stone for bashing

How to do Hapa Zome printing

1. Place your chopping board on the ground or on a sturdy table and put one piece of the fabric on top of it, with the side that you want to print on facing upwards.

2. Arrange the flowers and leaves face down onto the fabric. Place the other piece of fabric on top.

3. Take your rolling pin/mallet/stone and gently bash the top of the fabric all over so the flowers and leaves can make prints.

4. Carefully remove the top piece of fabric and leave the printed piece to dry, with the flowers and leaves still in place.

5. When it's dry, brush off the flowers and leaves.

6. Experiment by adding different patterns and colour combinations, and when you are happy with it ask a grown-up to iron the cloth to 'fix' it so the colours stay for longer.

> **Happiness is to hold flowers in both hands.**
> Japanese proverb

What to do with your Hapa Zome printing

You could use your cloth to make a piece of art, gift wrap, a flag or even to make bunting.

You can try Hapa Zome on watercolour paper too and make cards or bookmarks.

In spring the colours might be quite light – do you think they will be stronger in the summer?

Love

41

13 | Tremendous tree experiments

Trees are an amazing part of the natural world, but because we're so used to seeing them, we don't usually stop and think about just how wonderful they are.

Cool tree facts

• By studying fossils, scientists have estimated that trees have been on Earth for at least 370 million years.

• Trees produce oxygen, and help to reduce the amount of harmful carbon dioxide in our atmosphere.

• Trees can provide food, fuel, shelter and building materials.

• Some types of tree can live for thousands of years.

• Trees can defend themselves from insect attacks by producing chemicals that the insects dislike.

• They also use chemicals to communicate with other nearby trees, and to warn them of danger.

Try the four fun experiments on this page and the next to investigate trees in your area.

You will need

• A tape measure

• Paper

• A pencil

• Some trees to experiment on

Work out the age of a tree

1. Use a tape measure to measure around the tree's trunk, about one metre above the ground. This measurement is called the tree's girth.

2. Divide your girth measurement by the growth rate of the type of tree you have chosen. You can look this up online.

For example, an oak tree has an annual growth rate of 1.5 cm. If its girth is 75 cm, your sum is 75 divided by 1.5 which equals 50, so your tree is 50 years old.

Work out the height of a tree

1. Choose your tree, and stand with your back facing it.

2. Move your feet apart and keep your legs straight, then bend over and look between your legs.

3. Carefully move forwards or backwards, until you can see the top of the tree while you're bending over.

4. When you can just see the tree's top through your legs, measure the distance from your feet to the tree. This is roughly the same as the tree's height.

Read the rings of a tree stump

1. Count the rings on a tree stump to work out the tree's age before it fell. Each ring is equal to one year.

2. Narrow gaps between rings means there were a lack of water or nutrients that year.

3. Wide gaps between rings means there was plenty of water and nutrients that year.

Scientists use information like this to help them understand the effects of climate change on nature.

> Trees are poems that the Earth writes upon the sky.
> Kahlil Gibran

Forest bathing

Study the effect that trees can have on your mood. Forest bathing can help our bodies to relax and produce more of the chemicals that make us feel calm and happy.

1. Find a quiet spot in your local park or woodland where you are surrounded by trees.

2. Either walking slowly or sitting down, breathe deeply, and use your senses to explore the trees around you. What can you see, hear, touch, smell?

3. After you've done this for a few minutes, think about how you feel.

Summer

Welcome to summer, full of life and colour and with so many options for nature craft and play.

Summer days are perfect for being out and about in nature: crafting, playing, making and just being.

Summer is all about being active. You could have picnics, trips to the beach, bike rides. You can stay out later, playing games or making dens.

Flowers are blooming and it's the perfect time to press them, make flower crowns and even paint with them.

The natural world is buzzing with life this season. Insects, birds, butterflies and worms are all busy in our parks, gardens and woodlands.

Best of all, summer brings days and days off school so you can relax, explore or get creative. No more having to save it all up for the weekend!

Now's the time to be outside all the time!

14 | A creepy crawly scavenger hunt

There are lots of minibeasts out and about in summer, so here's a bug-themed scavenger hunt for you to have fun with.

You might spot little creatures in the garden, at the park or in the playground. Some like to hide away under stones, twigs or soil, so you'll probably have to do some detective work and look carefully to spot everything on the list.

There's no rush to complete it – you can keep coming back to your list, and if it takes all summer to find everything that's OK!

When you spot a creature on your list, have a think about why it might be where you found it. For example, is it safe, warm, quiet or a source of food? You could also look up your minibeast online to find out more about them.

In the shade and sun of grass blade forests, small living things had their metropolis.
Nancy Price

Snail

Ladybird

Bee

Ant

Caterpillar

Beetle

Butterfly

Worm

Slug

Centipede

Woodlouse

Spider

Crane fly

Moth

47

15 | Wonderful weeds

Weeds are the same as other plants – the only difference is that we don't usually want to grow them in our gardens. This might be because they like to crowd out other plants, or we don't like the way they look. But weeds can have lots of uses that are very important in nature. Dandelions are a brilliant example of this.

Amazing dandelion facts:

- Dandelions flower earlier than most plants, providing an important food source for bees in spring.

- The flower heads are very open, making it easy for pollinating insects to access pollen and nectar.

- Dandelion seeds are blown by the wind and can travel miles away from the plant.

- Every part of the plant is edible, and dandelions can also be used to make medicines and dyes.

- The name 'dandelion' is from the French for lion's tooth!

Next time you're out in nature, pick some dandelions and have a go at these fun activities.

Picking your dandelions

Try to pick your dandelions away from roads and the edges of paths, as these will have less dirt on them. You should also only pick a few dandelions at a time, leaving plenty for the bees.

Recipe for dandelion honey

Dandelion honey is a sweet treat that's vegan-and bee-friendly.

You will need

75 g dandelion flower heads

250 ml water

2 lemon slices

225 g sugar

A muslin cloth or fine sieve

A clean, empty jam jar with a lid

How to make...

1. Soak your dandelions in some cold water for ten minutes, to give any insects time to leave.

2. Drain the water off, then put the dandelions in a saucepan with the water and lemon. Bring to a boil, then turn the heat down and simmer for about 20 minutes.

3. Turn off the heat and leave your mixture to cool overnight.

4. Strain the mixture through the muslin cloth or sieve, then put the liquid back in the pan.

5. Add the sugar and heat gently until it dissolves.

6. Bring the liquid to a boil, reduce the heat and simmer for about 30 minutes.

7. Your dandelion honey is ready when it thickens up and looks like syrup.

8. Pour your honey into the jam jar. Once it has cooled down, keep it in the fridge.

Keep safe

Always ask a grown-up to help when you're working with hot liquids.

49

Make dandelion play dough

You can use dandelion flowers to make a natural dye for this fun home-made play dough.

You will need

About 30 dandelion flower heads

300 ml boiling water

130 g salt

2 tbsp vegetable oil

270 g flour

1 tbsp cream of tartar

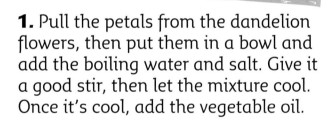

1. Pull the petals from the dandelion flowers, then put them in a bowl and add the boiling water and salt. Give it a good stir, then let the mixture cool. Once it's cool, add the vegetable oil.

2. Put the flour and cream of tartar in a mixing bowl and stir them together.

3. Pour your cooled dandelion mixture into your mixing bowl and stir, then use your hands to knead it into a smooth dough. If it's a bit sticky, add more flour a spoonful at a time.

4. Have fun with your nature-inspired play dough.

Create dandelion jewellery

It's not just daisies that make brilliant chains – dandelions are perfect too.

1. Pick a handful of dandelion flowers with the stalks attached.

2. Use your nail to make a small slit near the bottom of a stalk.

3. Pull another stalk through the slit until the flower head sits nicely against the first stalk.

4. Keep doing this until your chain is long enough to wear. Fasten the two ends together by tying them gently into a knot or twisting them around each other.

5. You could make a necklace, a bracelet or even a head garland.

Write a secret message

Dandelion stems contain sap. This is clear while it's wet, but it turns brown when it dries, so you can use it to write secret messages.

1. Pick a dandelion flower at the base of the stalk, where it meets the leaves. You should be able to see sap at the end of the stem.

2. Hold the stalk like a pencil and use the sap end to write your message on a piece of paper.

3. If your sap runs out, snap a little bit of the stem off. The new end will have more sap on it.

4. Your paper will look blank at first, but once the sap dries your message will be revealed!

16 A flower crown for the summer solstice

Summer solstice is an ancient festival which is celebrated all around the world. In the northern hemisphere, it happens between 20-22 June, which is the longest day of the year, when we have the most hours of daylight.

Summer solstice is a celebration of nature and the natural rhythm of the seasons. Traditionally people have marked this important day by watching the sun rise, collecting flowers and herbs, building a bonfire and dancing.

A great way to combine some of these traditions is to use flowers and greenery from a garden to make a flower crown.

You will need

- Some flowers with long stems

- Lengths of leafy foliage such as ivy

- A pre-made natural willow twig wreath (optional)

Picking your flowers and foliage

A garden is the best place to pick things for your crown. Before you start, ask the person whose garden it is which plants are OK to pick.

Flowers with long stems work well because you can twist them together. If you don't have any of these, try making daisy chains or dandelion chains to create longer lengths.

How to make a flower crown

1. Start with two long-stemmed flowers or pieces of foliage. Twist one end of each together to make one longer piece. You might need to make a simple knot with the ends, or tuck them under each other as you wrap them around.

2. Keep adding pieces of foliage or flowers to the ends, until you have a piece that's long enough to fit around your head with about 8 cm spare.

3. Twist the ends together to make a circle. Check if the crown fits, and adjust the length if you need to.

4. You can make your crown as simple or as elaborate as you like. Once you have your basic circle shape, you can weave more flowers, leaves and nature treasure into it.

5. For an easier flower crown, use a pre-made natural willow twig wreath and simply tuck your flowers and foliage into it.

6. Wear your crown and act like nature royalty!

Tips and ideas

Can you think of some other ways to celebrate nature for summer solstice? For example, you could write a poem, create a mandala, or make a list of all the amazing things you see in nature today.

If you've used a willow wreath to make your crown, you can use it over and over again to make more crowns – or even hang it up on your front door as a decoration.

53

17 | Make a sundial

A sundial is simply a device that uses the sun to show the time. People have been using this method since ancient times. It is an easy, and amazingly accurate, way to tell the time.

When the sun moves across the sky, its shadow moves too. A sundial uses the position of the shadow to show what time it is.

You will need

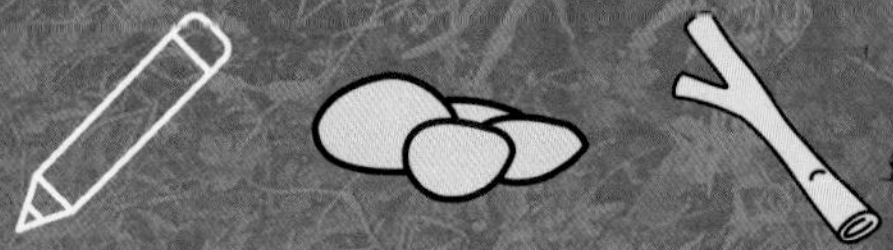

- 12 stones marked 1–12 with a Sharpie™, felt tip pen or paint (you can varnish them if you want to weatherproof them)

- 1 medium-sized stick (about 50 cm long)

- A sunny day

- A watch

54

How to make a sundial

1. Find a sunny spot outside to plant the stick, and push it hard into the grass or soil. Use a bucket with gravel or sand in if you don't have any earth to plant your stick in. Make sure the stick is vertical.

2. Start at midday. As the sun shines down on it, your stick will cast a shadow. Use the stone numbered 12 to mark where the end of the shadow falls on the ground and indicate 12 o'clock.

3. Return to the stick on the hour every hour (you might want to set an alarm to remind you) and use the correctly numbered stone to mark where the end of the stick's shadow falls. Do this until the sun goes down.

4. Next day start at 7 am and continue adding your stones till noon.

5. Add the stones for the night-time hours at even spaces to complete the dial around the stick.

As long as the sun shines, your sundial will be able to tell you what time of the day it is.

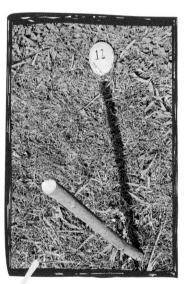

18 | Plant an amazing hanging basket

A hanging basket is a great way to grow lots of lovely plants in summer, even if you don't have a garden. You can hang one outside your front door, or somewhere you can see it from inside the house.

Some ideas for edible hanging baskets:
- A mini herb garden
- A lovely leafy salad basket with lettuce and trailing tomatoes
- Plants with edible flowers such as nasturtiums, pansies and cornflowers
- A fruity basket of strawberries

Some ideas for flowering hanging baskets:
- Summer bedding plants with flowers in your favourite colour
- A combination of plants that trail over the edge and grow upwards
- A 'hanging basket' plant selection – you can buy these from garden centres
- Any summer bedding plants your grown-ups have left over

You will need

- An empty hanging basket
- Some compost
- A selection of small plants
- A pair of gardening gloves
- A hand trowel

How to plant a hanging basket
1. If your basket has a round base, sit it on top of an empty plant pot or small bucket to stop it moving while you plant.

2. Add compost to your basket until it's almost full.

3. Carefully take each plant out of its pot by sliding your fingers around the plant's base, tipping it over and pulling the pot off.

4. Turn the plant the right way up and position it in your basket. If you're growing trailing plants, put these near the edges so they can tumble over.

56

> He who plants a garden plants happiness.
> Chinese proverb

5. Keep adding plants to your basket until it looks nice and full. When you've finished, fill in any gaps with compost.

6. Finish by watering your basket and hanging it up.

7. Plants grown in containers can dry out quickly in summer. Every couple of days, check if your basket needs a drink by poking a finger into the compost. If it feels dry, you need to water it.

Tips and ideas
Can you spot any wildlife enjoying your hanging basket plants and flowers?

If you've grown an edible hanging basket, what does your homegrown harvest taste like – is it fresher or tastier than when you buy it from a shop? Why do you think this is?

Keep safe
Always wear gloves when you're gardening, and wash your hands when you've finished.

19 | Butterfly SOS

Over recent years, the number of butterflies in our countryside and gardens has declined. This decrease is due to pollution, people using pesticides on crops and other plants, and more and more of the countryside being built on. If we want to keep our environment healthy, we need to do something to save the butterflies.

Whether you have a garden or simply a window box, there are lots of things you can do to help.

How to help the butterflies
1. Plant flowers that they love, especially nasturtiums, bluebells, lavender, cornflower, primroses and buddleia.

2. Leave out fruit for them to eat, such as overripe pears, plums or apples. You can use fruit from your fruit bowl or simply leave fruit where it is when it's fallen from a tree.

3. Don't use chemical sprays on plants that are flowering.

4. You could leave a little area of your garden purposefully wild with long grass and wildflowers.

5. You could also make the butterflies their own little paddling pool and feeder.

Make a butterfly pool
Butterflies love to land in puddles and drink up wet soil that contains lots of the nutrients they need.

You can make a 'puddling pool' for the butterflies by mixing soil with water in a shallow bowl or tub.

Put it by your colourful flowers, in the shade as much as possible, and keep adding water as it starts to dry out.

Make a butterfly feeder
The best food for butterflies is flowers, but you can also make them a feeder too.

You will need

- A plastic plate or lid
- Some string
- Strong sticky tape or a hole punch
- Overripe fruit (such as bananas, oranges or plums)
- Orange juice
- Coloured beads (optional)

How to make a butterfly feeder

1. Use the string to make a hanger for your plate by taping four long pieces to the underneath side, forming a cross shape from the centre of the plate. With the ice-cream tub lid you could punch a hole in each corner and tie a piece of string through each one.

2. You can decorate the strings with colourful beads if you want. This will help to attract the butterflies. Gather the other ends of the strings together at the top and tie them in a knot.

3. Hang your feeder from a tree branch.

4. Mash up the fruit then dollop it onto the plate along with some squirts of orange juice to stop it getting dry. Butterflies like all sorts of overripe fruit.

How many different types of butterfly can you spot in the garden, and which flowers do they appear to like the most?

Did you know?
Butterflies tend to be *diurnal* which means they are active during the day, whereas moths tend to be a duller colour and are *nocturnal*, which means active at night.

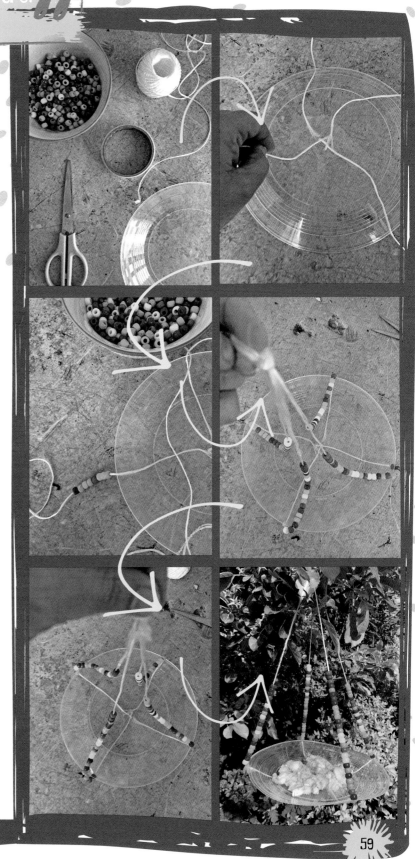

20 Painting with nature

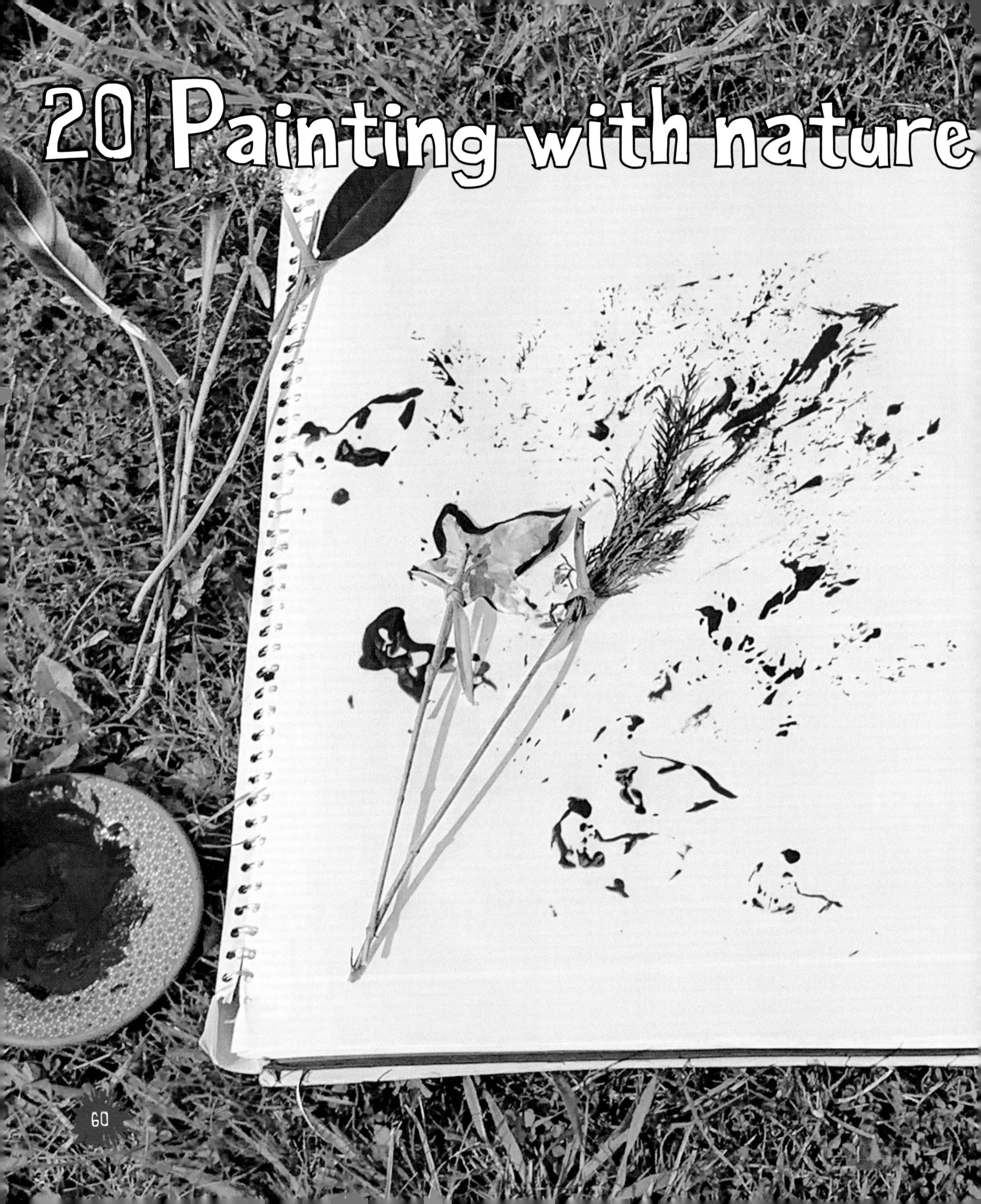

You don't need to go shopping for paintbrushes and paint when nature can provide you with all you need.

How to make natural paintbrushes

You will need

- fallen flowers, feathers and leaves of various sizes and shapes

- some sticks

- string

As you gather up your materials, have a think about what leaves or flowers would make interesting paintbrushes and the kind of prints, shapes and textures they would make.

Choose a stick that's the right length and thickness for the brush you're making (you can snap the stick down to size if you need to).

Attach a flower, feather or leaf to the stick with string. Alternatively for the leaf, you could just poke the stick through it. Pop your brushes into a jam jar once you've made them, ready to use.

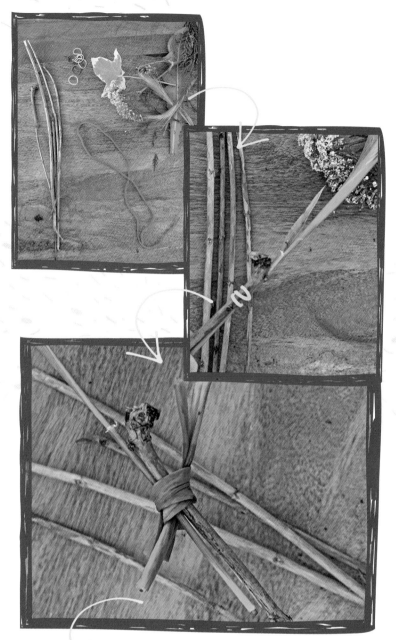

61

Now let's make some natural paint!

Paints are made from two things: pigment and a binder. The pigment provides the colour and the binder helps the colour stick to your paper or canvas.

For red: Try squishing a raspberry or strawberry through a sieve and adding a few drops of water and ½ teaspoon of flour.

For yellow: You could mash up some dandelions and buttercups (not the stalks though!), add a little water and leave it for a few hours.

For green: Try adding a tiny bit of hot water to spinach leaves. You could experiment with other leaves too.

For blue: Try adding a little water to crushed blue flower petals or blueberries.

For purple: Mash some blackberries through a sieve.

For brown: Use wet soil.

Here are some tips for making your paints:

• To thicken your paint, try adding ¼ teaspoon of flour (or more if required).

• You could add teeny tiny drops of honey to make your paints stick.

• To lighten your paints, you could add a squeeze of lemon juice (it's the acid in it that makes the paint go lighter).

• To darken your paints try adding a sprinkle of bicarbonate of soda (the alkali makes the paint go darker).

You can try lots of different things to make paint with, and experiment to get the colours and textures you want. You never know what might work until you try it, so get creative!

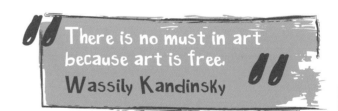

There is no must in art because art is free.
Wassily Kandinsky

63

21 | Cloud watching

Why cloud watch?
Clouds are all different shapes, sizes and even colours, and they are fascinating to watch. Cloud watching is deeply relaxing but it can also be a lot of fun, leading to the creation of the most amazing stories.

There are 35,000 members of the Cloud Appreciation Society, which shows how popular cloud watching is!

How to cloud watch
• Spread a blanket down on the ground outdoors and lie on your back for a while, watching as the clouds float by.

• Try to relax and give the clouds your full attention.

• Can you see them changing shape? Are they moving fast or slowly?

• Can you make out any objects in the clouds? Maybe the clouds are shaped like a dragon, or a mountain, or a boat? Let your imagination run wild!

• You might want to ask a friend or someone in your family to cloud watch with you, then you can try sharing the pictures you see with each other. Can you see what they see?

• You could link your cloud objects together and come up with an amazing story.

Do you know how clouds are made?
When water in lakes, rivers and oceans is heated up by the sun it turns into a gas called water vapour, which travels up to the sky in a process called evaporation. The higher it goes the cooler the temperature of the sky becomes, and as the water vapour cools down, it turns back into tiny water droplets. This is called condensation. The tiny water droplets high up in the sky are what make up the clouds.

> When you feel stuck, look at the sky. Clouds remind us that everything changes.
> Unknown

The colours of clouds

Did you know that clouds are white because they reflect the sun's light?

When they are full up with water (rain) and unable to reflect the sun's light they look grey.

Green clouds often mean a tornado is coming!

Spotting clouds

Here are the different types of clouds you might see when you're cloud watching – can you spot them all?

Tick each one off as you see it.

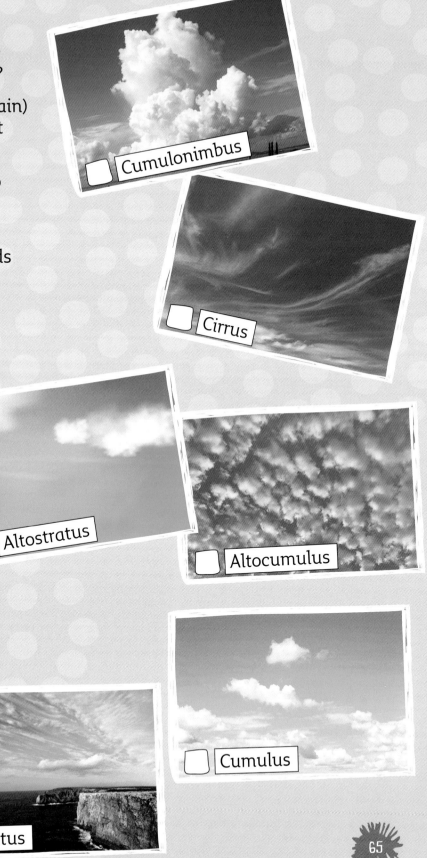

☐ Cumulonimbus

☐ Cirrus

☐ Cirrocumulus

☐ Altostratus

☐ Altocumulus

☐ Stratocumulus

☐ Stratus

☐ Cumulus

22 | Nature clay pressing

There are so many wonderful natural materials to collect in summer. Gather some nature treasures next time you go for a walk.

Collecting your nature treasures

You could search for nature treasures in your garden, local park, or woodland. Flowers, petals, leaves, feathers, seed pods and twigs are all great for pressing into clay.

Remember to look after nature by only collecting things from the ground, and not picking them from trees and plants.

You will need

- A variety of found nature treasures
- Some air-drying clay
- Greaseproof paper
- A rolling pin
- A blunt knife
- Cookie cutters (optional)
- Paint and paintbrush (optional)

How to make a nature clay pressing

1. You could make a big piece of clay art, or lots of smaller ones. Think about how big you want your art to be when deciding how much clay to use.

2. Put a sheet of greaseproof paper down on your work surface.

3. Use the rolling pin to roll out your clay until it is about 1 cm thick. If you like, you can use cookie cutters to shape it, or trim the edges with a knife.

4. Arrange your nature treasures on the surface of the clay.

5. Put another sheet of greaseproof paper on top.

6. Use your rolling pin to gently roll over the top of the clay so that the nature treasures are pressed in. Don't press down too hard.

7. Peel off the top sheet of greaseproof paper and remove your nature treasures.

8. If you want to hang up your clay pressing, poke a hole in it near the top.

9. Leave your clay to dry on a flat surface.

10. When your clay is dry, it's ready to display. You might like to add paint to show off the lovely nature imprints.

> *In nature, nothing is perfect and everything is perfect.*
> **Alice Walker**

Tips and ideas

How will you display your nature art? You could put it in a box frame, hang it up or simply stand it on a shelf. You could even make one for each season of the year and create a mini art gallery.

Nature clay pressings make fabulous home-made gifts – do you know someone who would love to receive one?

Keep safe

Wash your hands after collecting nature treasures, and never put anything you collect in your mouth.

Keep your hands flat when using your rolling pin, so that you don't trap your fingers.

Be careful when using your knife – you might need a grown-up to help you.

23 | The garden obstacle course challenge

One of the reasons why playing outdoors is so brilliant is that you can keep it very simple. Making a garden obstacle course is really quick and easy, and lots of fun – and you can use whatever is already there in the garden.

You will need

● Outdoor toys and play equipment

How to make a garden obstacle course

There are no rules here! Use the outdoor toys and play equipment to create your own unique obstacle course, and let your imagination run wild.

To get you started, here are some ideas:

● Cones or markers to dribble a football around

● A skipping rope to skip with, or use as a ground-level tightrope

● A hurdle to jump over, made from garden canes and string or buckets and a broom

● Hula hoops to jump through, throw over a target, or hula with

● A plank of wood to walk along

● An old sheet pinned down with tent pegs to crawl under

● A bucket to throw a ball into

● Goalposts to kick a ball between

● Stepping stones made from bricks or pieces of cardboard

● A section where you have to hop, skip or jump

● A cardboard box opened at the ends to make a crawl tunnel

● A paddling pool to fish something out of

● A sprinkler to run past without getting wet

● A water pistol tin can alley

● If there's a slide, trampoline or climbing frame you could use that too!

Tips and ideas

Think about the layout of your course before you start – how much space does each activity need? You can move things around as you build your course, until everything works really well together.

You might also like to think about your obstacle course rules. For example, if you fall off a balance beam, you have to go back to the start of the beam and try again. It might help to have a go at your course before working these out.

If there are lots of you playing, you could split up into teams and tackle the obstacle course as a relay race.

To give yourself a challenge, ask someone to time you on the obstacle course, and then try to beat your time. Perhaps you can persuade the grown-ups to have a go too!

Keep safe
Always check with a grown-up before borrowing things to make your obstacle course.

24 | Make a twig boat

Twig boats are great fun to make as well as to sail. They float brilliantly.

You will need

- Some long pieces of tough grass (you may need to experiment with different types – montbretia leaves were used in the end). You can use string if you can't find any long grass.

- 6 twigs, broken into pieces of similar lengths

- A leaf

- A few fallen flowers

How to make a twig boat
1. Lay out the pieces of grass, then place the twigs on top of them, at right angles to the grass. The sticks need to be close together.

2. Tightly wrap the grass around the twigs to bring them together, then tie the two ends of each piece of grass together with a knot. It may take a few attempts to get this right.

3. Try to keep your twigs flat and as tight together as possible.

4. Next, take one extra twig and slot it into the bottom of your boat to become the mast.

5. To make the sail, thread a leaf gently onto the mast by poking the end of the mast through the leaf in two places.

6. Add a few fallen tiny flowers for decoration and that's it!

7. Set your twig boat afloat in a paddling pool, bathtub or shallow stream.

Could you make a few and have races with your friends?

Keep safe
Never set your boat in flowing water without a grown-up present, as water can be dangerous.

There is nothing — absolutely nothing — half so much worth doing as simply messing about in boats. "
Kenneth Grahame

25 | Outdoor games to play with friends

The outdoors really is the most amazing playground. Green spaces are perfect for playing all kinds of exciting games, and you don't need any fancy equipment.

Meet your friends in your local park or field and have some fun with these outdoor games.

Red Light, Green Light

1. One person is the traffic light, and stands at one end of the space. Everyone else stands at the other end.

2. The player who is the traffic light starts with their back to the group. Everyone else tries to get closer to the traffic light while they are not looking.

3. The traffic light can turn round at any point and say, 'Red Light!' When this happens, everyone else has to freeze. If someone is spotted moving, they have to go back to the start.

4. When the traffic light turns their back, they have to say, 'Green Light!' and everyone can try to creep closer.

5. The winner is the first player to reach the traffic light and tag them. The winner becomes traffic light next.

Capture the Flag

1. Divide the players into two teams.

2. Agree on the boundaries for the game, and split the playing area in half – you could use markers to help show where these are.

3. Each team has a half, and decides where to place their 'flag' (this can be any object) and their jail.

4. Each team starts in their own half. The aim is to capture the other team's flag.

5. When the game begins, everyone tries to reach the other team's flag without being caught.

6. If a team member is caught while they are in the other team's half, they are sent to jail. They have to stay there until one of their team frees them by touching them. Once freed they can return to their half, and can't be caught again on the way there.

7. The first team to capture the other team's flag and return it to their own half is the winner.

Spud

1. One player is 'it', and all the other players are given a number, starting with 1.

2. The player who is 'it' throws a ball up in the air while everyone else runs away.

3. As the ball goes up, the player who is 'it' shouts out one of the numbers, then runs away.

4. The player with that number has to run back and grab the ball. Once they have it, they shout, 'Spud!' and everyone else has to freeze.

5. The player with the ball tries to hit another player with the ball, aiming below the waist. The frozen player can't move their feet, but can try to dodge the ball. If the ball hits them, they become 'it' and get a letter, starting with 'S', then 'P', then 'U', then 'D'. If the ball misses them or they catch it, the player who threw the ball becomes 'it' and gets a letter.

6. If a player gets all four letters to spell SPUD, they are out.

> Play is the highest form of research.
> Albert Einstein

26|50 things to do at the seaside

A bumper list of fun things you can do at the beach...

1. Go fossil hunting

2. Build a big sandcastle on the shoreline as the tide is coming in, and see how long it can survive against the waves

3. Dig for worms where you see the curly-wurly lines in the sand, but don't disturb them!

4. Play I-spy

5. Take a camera so you can make a scrapbook of photos of all the interesting things you see

6. Find a small shell with a hole in it and string it onto a piece of ribbon or twine to make a pretty bracelet or necklace

7. Make sand angels

8. Use a metal detector to hunt for treasure

9. Create 'land art' with shells and stones

10. Make sand hurdles – little piles of sand to jump over

11. Play a game like cricket, rounders, frisbee or football!

12. Go wave jumping (holding hands with a grown-up)

13. Create pictures of people with seaweed for hair, shells for noses and pebbles for their eyes

14. Follow animal tracks

15. Build sandcastles

16. Paddle in the water

17. Search for sea glass

18. Have a long jump competition

19. Write your name in the sand

20. Skim stones on the water

21. Roll down the sand dunes

22. Play tic tac toe by drawing lines in the sand and using shells and stones as noughts and crosses

23. Grab a handful of stones and have a competition to see who can be the first to hit a large pebble

24. Go rock pooling

25. Create a scavenger hunt! Make a list of beachy items to find and race to see who finds them all first

26. Make a tower out of pebbles

27. Fly a kite

28. Dig a hole in the sand so deep that it fills with water

29. See who can find the biggest shell

30. Bury a family member in the sand (but make sure you leave their head poking out!)

31. See the sun rise

32. Watch the sun set

33. Go bodyboarding

34. Make a beach jar filled with sand and a few little treasures you find

35. Make a beach mandala with pebbles, shells, seaweed or sticks

36. Have a family beach Olympics (think relay races with buckets of water and jumping over spades)

37. Make a waterway and a fort in the sand, ready for the tide coming in

38. Look for crabs

39. Go for a walk

40. Watch the sky

41. Take binoculars and follow the seagulls

42. Use a snorkel or goggles so you can see under the water

43. Research the tide times and watch them come in and out

44. Look at where you are on a map and work out what lies beyond the horizon

45. Read a book and relax

46. Have a beach clean-up!

47. Go to the beach at night and see the stars

48. Do some creative writing inspired by the sea

49. Have a delicious picnic

50. Visit the local lifeboat

Happiness is a day at the beach.
Unknown

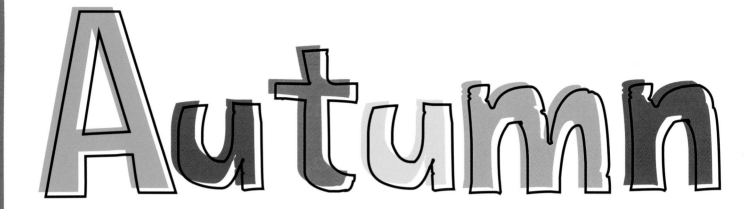

Autumn

Autumn means the end of summer and going back to school, so you might not think it is the best of seasons...

But autumn is wonderful! So many amazing changes take place in nature and there are so many treasures to be found that it's a great time to get crafting and making art from nature.

Trees shower us with acorns, pine cones and conkers, and drop whirling colourful leaves around our heads. Their branches hang low with fruits ripe for picking.

The animal kingdom gives us awesome gifts such as spiders' webs and fallen feathers. The trees bend low with blackberries and apples ripe for picking and send whirling colourful leaves around our heads.

Autumn also brings us Harvest, Halloween and Bonfire Night, which inspire us to be creative.

There are a few gardening projects to be getting on with too, with planning and planting for the year ahead.

It's going to be a busy and beautiful season! Keep going outside, just wrap up a bit warmer and find your wellies.

27 | Make a journey stick

A journey stick is a fun way to record a nature walk, using fallen nature treasure that you collect along the way.

Journey sticks have been around for a very long time. Native Americans and Aboriginal people used them to track their journeys and tell stories about their travels.

You will need

- A stick

- A piece of string or wool or a strip of cardboard

- Double-sided sticky tape

How to make a journey stick

1. Start by finding your stick. You can choose any length, but think about how long your walk is going to be. Longer walks might need a longer stick!

2. Tie one end of your string to the top of your stick.

3. If you're using cardboard, attach a length of double-sided sticky tape to one side.

4. During your walk, look out for nature treasure. When you find something that you'd like to add to your stick, use the string or sticky tape to attach it, working down the stick as you go. Seed pods, leaves, petals, feathers, berries and twigs all work really well.

Make sure you only collect nature treasure that has fallen to the ground – don't pick things from plants and trees.

5. When you've finished your walk you will have a lovely record of the nature you saw along the way.

Tips and ideas

Journey sticks are great starting points for storytelling. What story is your journey stick telling? Let your imagination run wild!

Could you make a journey stick on the same walk in a different season, and compare the two?

How about making a journey stick with a particular theme? For example, all leaves, or a particular colour.

Keep safe

When you have finished collecting your nature treasures, keep your hands away from your face and wash them when you get home.

Never put any nature treasures in your mouth.

" In every walk with nature one receives far more than he seeks "
John Muir

28 | Painted Feather Mobile

You will find lots of feathers lying around in early autumn. Birds lose their feathers in late summer so that they can grow stronger, warmer ones to see them through the wintertime.

It takes a lot of energy to fly when feathers have been lost, and even more energy to grow new ones, so whilst this is happening birds can't fly away so easily from predators. In order to stay safe, they hide away for a while.

You might miss the birds singing in early September but their feathers are a lovely thing to collect whilst you are out on your nature walks.

They look beautiful displayed naturally in a jar till you are ready to use them, and they make such a brilliant craft material you'll be really pleased you picked them up. You will be able to use your feathers for lots of projects over the next few months so gather in quite a few.

It is not enough to have the feathers. You must dare to fly.
Cass van Krah

You will need

- Found feathers of any kind
- Small thin paintbrush
- Water
- Acrylic paint
- String twine or wool
- A stick or branch
- A painting mat or tray

Gathering your supplies
Find a branch or a strong stick from which you can hang your feathers.

Collect a selection of feathers and handle them gently so they don't break. It is important to give the feathers a good clean. See page 11 for how to do this.

How to make a painted feather mobile
1. Once the feathers have been washed and dried, lay them on the mat or tray.

2. Decide on your colour scheme.

3. Use a brush to apply the paint, in the direction of the feathers.

4. When the paint has dried, turn the feather over and do the other side.

5. Once both sides are dry, you can add white or black dots or glitter glue to make patterns, or leave them plain.

6. When you are finished, tie various lengths of string to the stick, then tie the other end around the base of the feather.

Keep safe
Make sure you wash your hands really well after handling the feathers.

29 | Go Brambling

People have enjoyed brambling (blackberry picking) for thousands of years. It is like treasure hunting – at first you might not find any at all, then suddenly there are loads.

Blackberries are easy to identify, high in vitamin C, which helps you ward off colds, and they taste delicious! The best places to find them are around allotments, beside canals, in woodlands and in hedges.

You will need

- Plastic food box with a lid, or a deep bowl

- Gloves (optional)

How to pick blackberries

When a blackberry is ready to pick, it will be black and shiny and will easily pull away from the plant. Just give it a gentle tug. Be very gentle when putting your blackberries in their box or they will squish, break and bruise. Leave any that are red or firm, or not pulling away easily, where they are.

Tips and ideas

Only take as many as you need so there is enough for everyone and the fruit doesn't get wasted. Make sure there is enough left for the birds too as they help to spread the seeds which grow into new plants.

Give your blackberries a wash before you eat them, by swirling them in a bowl of clean water rather than holding them under a running top, as that would crush them. Remove any little stalks too.

Keep safe

If you aren't certain that what you are picking is a blackberry, then don't pick it. There are other types of berry that are poisonous and could make you sick, so you need to be sure.

Wash your hands after picking the blackberries.

And mind out for thorns!

> "Live in each season as it passes: breathe the air, drink the drink, taste the fruit."
> Henry David Thoreau

Recipe for blackberry and apple crumble

Blackberries can be eaten on their own, or heated up and served with a little ice-cream. Or you might want to make this blackberry and apple crumble.

You will need
For the filling
- 4 large apples of any kind
- 200 g blackberries
- 3 tablespoons brown sugar
- 2 teaspoons ground cinnamon

For the crumble topping
- 250 g plain flour
- 50 g rolled oats
- 150 g sugar
- 200 g butter/Dairy-free spread

Prep
Preheat the oven to 180°C /gas mark 4 and weigh out all your ingredients; wash your hands, pop on your apron and you're ready to go.

Prepare the filling
1. Wash your fruit gently, chop up your apples, then lay it all out on the bottom of an ovenproof dish.

2. Stir the sugar and cinnamon gently into the fruit so it is all covered.

Make the crumble topping
1. Mix together the flour, oats and sugar in a large bowl. Next rub the butter into the mix with your fingertips till it looks like breadcrumbs.

2. Sprinkle your crumble mix over the fruit – but don't press it down. Make sure all the fruit is covered.

How to bake it
Bake in the oven for 40 minutes. Check after 30 minutes and, if the top is getting brown turn, the heat down to 160°C / gas mark 3.

This crumble will taste delicious with custard or cream or even on its own!

84

It's the PERFECT pud for autumn.

85

30|Conker fun

In autumn lots of trees are dropping their seeds. Some of the fallen seeds will sprout into new little trees, and some will be eaten by wildlife.

Conkers are the seeds produced by horse chestnut trees. Collecting conkers is a fun thing to do when you're out on a walk. You can turn them into conker creatures or play a game with them.

You will need

- Conkers in various shapes and sizes
- Blunt darning needle
- Wooden cocktail sticks or wooden craft matchsticks
- Acrylic paint or permanent markers
- String
- Scissors
- Pipe cleaners (optional)
- Tissue paper (optional)
- Googly eyes (optional)

Gathering your conkers

Horse chestnut trees are often found in parks and woodland areas. You might already know where to find one near you, but if not you could ask a grown-up to help. If you're not sure how to spot a horse chestnut tree, look up what their leaves are like before you head outside.

The best time of year to find conkers is usually early autumn. They will be lying on the ground around the trunk of the tree.

Choose conkers that are firm, shiny and undamaged. You might like to take a little bag with you to carry them in.

Keep safe

Don't try to pick up conkers that have fallen onto the road.

When you have finished collecting your conkers, keep your hands away from your face and wash them when you get home.

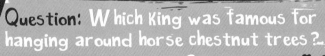

Question: Which king was famous for hanging around horse chestnut trees?
Answer: William the Conker-er.

How to make conker creatures

You can connect conkers together or paint them to make your very own conker creatures.

1. To connect two conkers together, make a small hole in each one with a cocktail stick or a blunt needle. Be careful when you do this – you might need to ask a grown-up for help.

2. Push a cocktail stick or matchstick into one hole, then push the other end into the hole in your other conker to connect them. Sticks also make brilliant legs, arms, whiskers, hair and ears.

3. Use acrylic paint or permanent markers to add detail to your creature.

4. You can also use other craft supplies to decorate your conker creature. Pipe cleaners, tissue paper and googly eyes all work well.

5. You can also make a hole all the way through a conker and thread string through it. This is a great way to make conker snakes and caterpillars – or even a necklace.

You don't have to make a real animal, let your imagination run wild and see what you end up with!

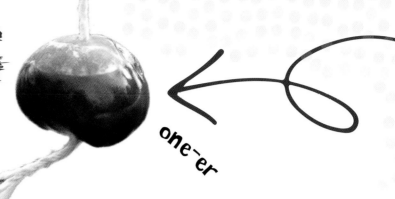

one-er

How to play conkers

Before you can play, you need to thread your conker onto a piece of string. Ask a grown-up to help you make a hole all the way through from top to bottom, using a blunt needle or skewer.

Thread a piece of string through your conker, and tie a double knot at the bottom so the conker hangs on the string.

Rules

You need two people to play it.

Each player has their own conker on a string. Take it in turns to use your conker to hit your opponent's conker. The person who isn't doing the hitting must hold their string up so their conker hangs down.

Try wrapping the string around your hand a few times before taking aim. When you're ready, hold the conker in your other hand and pull it back, then swing it down.

If you miss, you can have up to two more goes before it's your opponent's turn.

If your strings get tangled up, the first player to shout **'Strings!'** gets an extra shot.

The winner is the first player to knock their opponent's conker off its string.

The winning conker will then have a score of 1 and is known as a **'one-er'**. If it then beats another conker, it becomes a **'two-er'** and so on. If you beat a conker that already has a higher score than 1, you add all of that score to your conker.

Top tips

The best conkers to use are firm and symmetrical. Choose one that looks nice and strong. A damaged conker will float in water, so you could do this test too.

Conkers can hurt if they hit you. If you're playing conkers, be careful when you swing your conker at your opponent, and make sure your string isn't long enough to hit them.

Tips and ideas

If you plant a conker in the ground, it grows into a horse chestnut tree. You could have a go, but bear in mind it might grow into a really big tree!

31 | Plant a bulb lasagne

Autumn is the perfect time of year to plant spring bulbs. They stay under the ground all winter, and in spring they grow into gorgeous flowers.

Spring bulbs are happy growing in pots, so you don't even need a garden to grow them. A bulb lasagne is a clever way of doing this. You plant the bulbs in layers, which is a bit like making a lasagne with layers of different ingredients – hence the name. This means that when the first bulbs have finished flowering, the next layer will flower, and so on, giving you a succession of lovely flowers.

You will need

- A container
- Some compost
- Gardening gloves
- A hand trowel
- A variety of spring bulbs.

When you're choosing your spring bulbs, check the flowering month on the packet and try to choose bulbs that flower in different months.

Here are some ideas to help you:
Bottom layer: *tulips, hyacinths*
Middle layer: *daffodils, muscari* (also called grape hyacinths)
Top layer: *crocus, miniature iris*

How to plant a bulb lasagne
1. Lay out your bulbs in the order that you're going to plant them. The first ones to plant will be the bulbs that flower last, followed by the bulbs that flower before them, and so on. The bulbs on the top layer will be the ones that are going to flower first.

2. Add some compost to your pot until it's about one third full.

3. Gently push your last flowering bulbs into the compost. The pointy end of the bulb should be pointing upwards. Leave a bit of room around each bulb.

4. Cover your bulbs with a layer of compost, then plant your variety of bulbs that flower before the bottom bulbs on top.

5. Add another layer of compost to your container, then plant your bulbs that will flower first at the top.

6. Cover your top layer of bulbs with compost.

7. When you've finished planting, water your container.

Tips and ideas
Where will you put your bulb lasagne? Choose a spot that you walk past regularly and you'll be able to enjoy the flowers more often.

How does seeing the colourful flowers make you feel?

Could you plant a bulb lasagne for someone you know who doesn't have a garden?

Keep safe
• Always wear gloves when handling bulbs as some types can irritate your skin.

• Never put bulbs in your mouth – some are poisonous.

• Wash your hands when you've finished planting your bulb lasagne.

"The glory of gardening: hands in the dirt, head in the sun, heart with nature."
Alfred Austin

32 | Collect seeds

Plants are very clever. Their flowers produce seeds, which can grow into a whole new generation of plants.

Flowers need to be pollinated so that they can make seeds. Plants do this by using insects, birds, bats, small animals and the wind to move their pollen from one flower to another.

Once they're ready, the seeds will fall from the flower, be blown away by the wind or be carried away by wildlife.

You will need

- Paper bags or paper envelopes
- A pen or pencil
- Scissors or secateurs

How to collect seeds

1. Choose a dry, calm day to collect your seeds. Seeds that are dry will be more likely to grow when you plant them, and they store well if you don't want to plant them straight away.

2. Walk around your garden, looking out for plants with flowers that look dry and dead. If the flowers are still blooming on a plant, you need to wait a bit longer for the seeds to be ready.

3. Lots of plants make their seeds at the centre of the flower heads, but some make them in pods which hang on the plant.

To collect seeds from a flower head, you can snip off the whole flower and shake the seeds into your paper bag. Another way to do it is to put one hand underneath a flower on the plant, and use your fingers to rub the seed head until the seeds fall onto your palm.

To collect seeds from a seed pod, snip the pod off the plant and open it up to remove the seeds.

4. When you've finished collecting your seeds, write the name of the plant on your paper bag.

5. You can plant your seeds straight away, or save them for later. Keep your paper bag somewhere dry and cool until you're ready to use them.

Tips and ideas

Try to leave some flowers on your plants, these will provide a source of food and shelter over the winter for local birds and wildlife.

If you don't have a garden, does someone else in your family have one that you could collect seeds from? Perhaps your school has a garden that you could use? Or you could find out if there is a community garden close to where you live.

Could you share some of your seeds with friends and neighbours? This is called a seed swap, and is a fun way to grow types of plants that you don't already have.

Keep safe

Scissors and secateurs are sharp, so be very careful if you're using them to snip off flower stems.

Don't ever eat any seeds that you collect, and wash your hands after handling them.

33 | Wildflower seed balls

A seed ball is a ball of soil and water with seeds inside that you throw. Seeds are really light, so if you threw them on their own they would blow away. The soil in a seed ball keeps the seeds together, protects them from animals and birds and gives them the food they need to begin to grow.

When you throw a seed ball and the seeds begin to grow, the ball will begin to break apart. The soil and water help the seeds grow into flowers.

You can throw these balls either into your garden or into any gloomy piece of public (not private) land.

They are best thrown in spring or autumn. It takes about three weeks for the seeds to wiggle through and take root in the ground.

> "The creation of a thousand forests is in one acorn.
> Ralph Waldo Emerson

Normally seeds are spread by the wind or water or through bird or animal poo. Throwing seed balls is a human way of spreading seeds. They can make areas look beautiful and they are great for wildlife.

You will need

- 3 cups of soil or compost
- 1 cup of plain flour
- Water
- A tray or bowl
- 1 packet of wildflower seeds

How to make wildflower seed balls

1. Mix the soil and flour together in a bowl and add splashes of water till the mixture is sticky but not too wet.

2. Mould your mixture into small balls about the size of a bouncy ball.

3. Lay out your seeds on a tray or in a bowl.

4. Roll your balls around the tray or bowl so they pick up the seeds.

5. Leave them to dry for 24 hours.

6. Go out and throw your seed balls!

Tips and ideas

Don't throw your seed balls onto someone's property without their permission. Instead, you could look for wasteland, neglected public flower beds, or perhaps the base of a tree on your street.

Keep safe

Don't wander onto derelict property or trespass on other people's property without consent.

Leaves make such fantastic crafting material. You could make leaf bunting, leaf animal pictures, leaf bowls – so many ideas! But Halloween is looming, so we are going to explore the spookier side of leaves.

Leaf bats

You could use your bats as decorations on a shelf, or you could attach a magnet and use them as fridge magnets.

You will need:

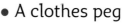

- A clothes peg
- Scissors
- Black paint
- Two identical leaves with jagged edges
- Little googly eyes (optional)

How to make a leaf bat

1. Preserve (page 10) your leaves first so they will last a while.

2. If you want to shape your leaves to look more like bat wings, layer your leaves on top of one another and cut them carefully with scissors.

3. Paint your leaves and peg on one side and leave them to dry.

4. Turn the leaves and peg over and paint the other sides.

5. Carefully secure your leaves in the closure of the peg and attach googly eyes.

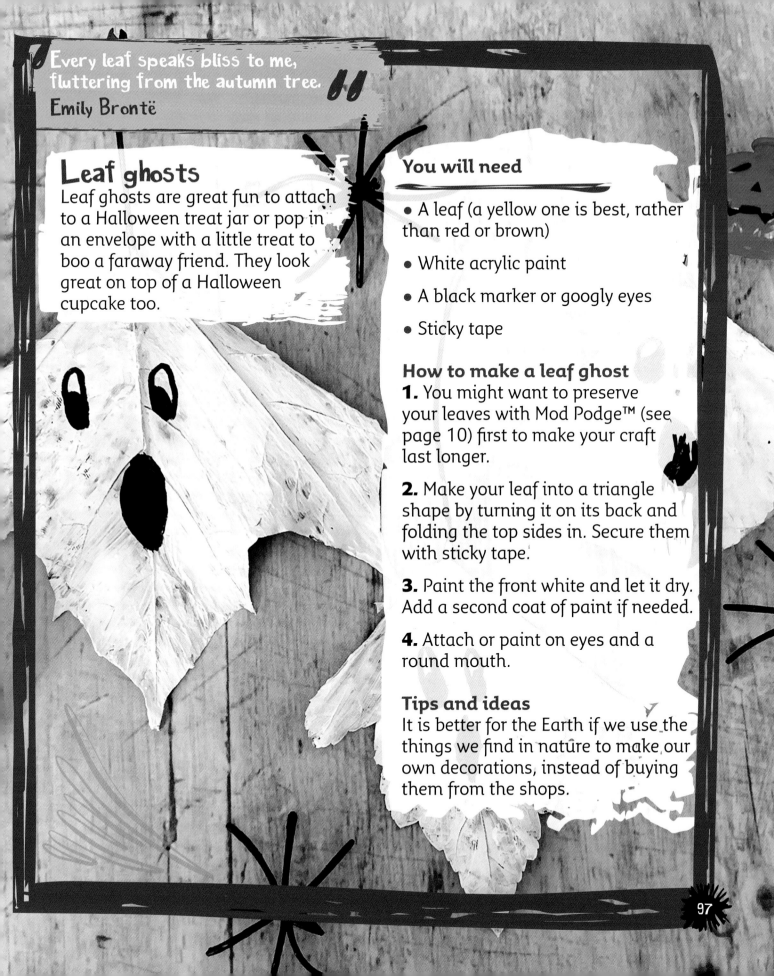

Leaf ghosts

Leaf ghosts are great fun to attach to a Halloween treat jar or pop in an envelope with a little treat to boo a faraway friend. They look great on top of a Halloween cupcake too.

You will need

- A leaf (a yellow one is best, rather than red or brown)

- White acrylic paint

- A black marker or googly eyes

- Sticky tape

How to make a leaf ghost

1. You might want to preserve your leaves with Mod Podge™ (see page 10) first to make your craft last longer.

2. Make your leaf into a triangle shape by turning it on its back and folding the top sides in. Secure them with sticky tape.

3. Paint the front white and let it dry. Add a second coat of paint if needed.

4. Attach or paint on eyes and a round mouth.

Tips and ideas

It is better for the Earth if we use the things we find in nature to make our own decorations, instead of buying them from the shops.

35 | Pumpkin fun

Paint your pumpkin

Instead of carving your pumpkin, you can paint it. Acrylic paint works best.

You could paint a spooky scene, create a repeating pattern, include words, or go abstract with lots of colours and shapes. Anything goes! Acrylic paint works best.

Eat your pumpkin

When you're preparing your pumpkin for carving, keep the seeds from the centre and roast them to eat. After Halloween, rather than simply throwing your pumpkin away, puree the flesh and use it to make pumpkin muffins, bread or soup.

Whatever you're making, first you will need to puree your pumpkin.

1. Line a baking tray with baking paper and heat your oven to 200°C / gas mark 6.

2. Rinse and dry the pumpkin and ask your grown-up to cut it in half.

3. Make sure all of the seeds and the stringy bits have been removed.

4. Bake the pumpkin in the oven for 45 minutes to 1 hour, until a knife slides easily into the flesh.

5. Let the pumpkin cool down, then scoop out the flesh and put it into a blender. Blend until really smooth.

Recipe for Pumpkin Muffins (makes 10)

You will need
For the muffins
- 125 g plain flour
- 1 teaspoon baking powder
- 1½ teaspoons ground cinnamon
- 1½ teaspoons ground ginger
- ½ teaspoon salt
- 2 large eggs
- 175 g light brown sugar
- 1 teaspoon vanilla extract
- 120 ml vegetable oil
- 220 g pumpkin puree
- A handful of chocolate chips (optional)

For the icing
- 100 g cream cheese
- 150 g soft butter
- 1 teaspoon vanilla extract
- 250 g icing sugar

Prep
1. Preheat your oven to 180°C / gas mark 4.

2. Place 10 muffin cases into a muffin tray.

Make the muffins
1. Combine the flour, baking powder, cinnamon, ginger and salt in a bowl.

2. In another bowl, whisk together the eggs, sugar, vanilla extract and vegetable oil.

3. Add the pumpkin puree to the egg mixture and whisk again.

4. Combine both mixtures and mix gently. Add the chocolate chips if you are using them.

5. Pour the mixture into the muffin cases and pop into the oven for 20 minutes. They are ready when an inserted knife or skewer comes out clean.

Make the icing
1. Cream together the cream cheese and butter, then add the vanilla extract.

2. Add the icing sugar a little at a time and keep stirring until the mixture is smooth.

3. Spread icing onto the muffins once they are completely cool.

Make your pumpkin into a bird feeder

Pumpkins are the perfect shape for a bird feeder. Birds will love to feast on the pumpkin, as well as the bird food inside it.

If you don't have a spare pumpkin, you can turn your Halloween pumpkin into a bird feeder once you've finished with it.

You will need

- A small pumpkin
- A large spoon
- A knife
- A skewer
- Some string
- Two sticks
- Bird seed

How to make a pumpkin bird feeder

1. Ask a grown-up to cut your pumpkin in half horizontally.

2. Scoop out the seeds and stringy bits from the bottom half of the pumpkin (you can use the top half to make your pumpkin muffins).

3. Ask a grown-up to use a skewer to make two holes opposite each other, about halfway down the side of the pumpkin. Repeat this step so that you have four holes equally spaced around the pumpkin. The holes need to be big enough to fit your sticks through.

4. Poke a stick through one of the holes, and then through the one on the opposite side. Do the same with the other stick through the remaining two holes, so that the sticks make a cross shape in the middle of the pumpkin.

5. Cut four pieces of string about 60 cm long. Tie a piece of string around each stick, where it meets the outside of the pumpkin. Make a double knot each time.

6. Tie all four pieces of string together at the other end. You might need to adjust the length of some pieces to make your pumpkin hang straight.

7. Fill your pumpkin with bird seed, and hang it up outside.

Tips and ideas

Who visits your pumpkin bird feeder? You could keep a record of the different types of bird.

Is your pumpkin feeder visited more at a particular time of day? Why do you think this is?

Perhaps you could hang your pumpkin feeder in your local park to give the wildlife that lives there an autumn treat. This is a great option if you don't have any trees or large bushes in your garden.

Keep safe

Make sure you ask a grown-up to cut your pumpkin and make the holes in it – don't try to do it yourself.

Birds might think bird seed is yummy, but remember it's designed for birds, not humans – don't ever eat it!

36 | Make a mandala

A mandala is a circular pattern with a design that grows out symmetrically from its centre. It comes from the ancient Sanskrit word for 'circle'.

You can find a lot of mandalas in nature. Try looking closely at spiders' webs and flowers, and the rings on a tree stump. You even have one in your eye.

Mindfulness and mandala making

Creating a mandala is an act of mindfulness. It takes a lot of concentration and you have to be focused. This can help you to distance yourself from any worries and feel calm. And by creating your mandala in a public place, you can share its beauty with other people too. Mandalas can be made in every season and every location. You could use spring flowers, shells on a beach in summer or perhaps berries, sticks and pine cones in winter.

You will need

Lots of fallen treasure, with at least two of each item so you can make a pattern. Items you might want to use include: leaves, sticks, old lavender, perhaps a sunflower head, acorns, broken pine cones, conkers, feathers... the items don't have to be perfect or unbroken to be part of something beautiful.

How to make a mandala

1. Gather in your treasures.

2. Find a clear space on the ground to set your mandala (avoid a path so no one walks on it).

3. Decide what to put in the centre then build your pattern around it.

Tips and ideas

• You can make a mandala out of stones, shells or leaves. It is art that you can make anywhere and everywhere.

• Mandalas can be made in every season and every location. You could use blossom and spring flowers, shells on a beach in summer, or in winter perhaps berries, sticks and pine cones.

• Working with friends, you could create a huge mandala.

Keep safe

While you are collecting your treasures, keep your hands away from your face and wash them when you get home.

> To the artist there is never anything ugly in nature.
> Auguste Rodin

103

Autumn Scavenger Hunt...

1 A noisy bird ☐
2 A conker ☐
3 Blackberries ☐
4 A pinecone ☐
5 Red leaf ☐
6 Orange leaf ☐
7 Yellow leaf ☐
8 Red or white berries ☐
9 2 feathers ☐
10 A flower ☐

11 A big puddle ☐
12 A spiders web ☐
13 A seed ☐
14 An acorn ☐
15 The sound of the wind ☐
16 An animal ☐
17 Something prickly ☐
18 A big stick ☐
19 A conker case ☐
20 A ... stone ☐

> **Not all treasure is silver and gold, mate.**
> Captain Jack Sparrow

Autumn is one of the very best times to go on a scavenger hunt. You can do this list on your own, in teams or as a family.

You don't have to bring home all the things you find on this list, spotting them is enough. Tick things off as you find them, hear them, feel them or see them.

How many can you find?

1. A noisy bird
2. A conker
3. Blackberries
4. A pine cone
5. A red leaf
6. An orange leaf
7. A yellow leaf
8. Red or white berries
9. Two feathers
10. A flower
11. A big puddle
12. A spider's web
13. A seed
14. An acorn
15. The sound of the wind
16. An animal
17. Something prickly
18. A big stick
19. A prickly conker case
20. A circular stone

How to make your scavenger list look amazing
Make the scavenger hunt list look old, so it feels like a proper treasure hunt.

You will need

- A teabag
- White Paper
- Water

How to make it
1. Dip the teabag into cold water then smear it over both sides of your piece of paper. Don't make it too wet or the paper will tear.

2. Leave it to dry tbefore writing your list.

3. Leave space next to each item so it can be ticked off as you find it.

38 | Make your own veggie creature

Autumn is a time of year when lots of fruit and vegetables are ready to harvest. As well as being tasty to eat, they're also perfect for turning into veggie creatures.

You can use whatever fruit and vegetables you have available at home.

You will need

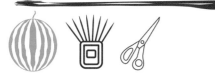

- A few different fruits and vegetables

- Wooden cocktail sticks or wooden craft matchsticks

- Scissors or a knife

How to make veggie creatures

Have a look at the shapes and sizes of your fruit and vegetables. Are some things obviously suited to being a particular body part? Could you use different parts of the fruit or vegetable in different ways?

Here are some tips to help get you started:
- Larger things like tomatoes, potatoes and apples make good bodies.

- Smaller things like berries and cherry tomatoes are great for noses, eyes and ears.

- You can cut a piece of fruit or vegetable into smaller, different-shaped pieces. This is great for adding detail to your creature. Stalks are also handy here.

- You can snip off leafy stems and use them to make hair, clothes, whiskers, or something for your creature to sit on.

Use a cocktail stick to connect pieces together. Push it gently into each piece to make a hole, then push the stick into the holes on each piece to connect them.

There are no rules for making your creatures – play around with shapes and designs as much as you want. You don't have to make a 'real' animal, get creative and see what works best with the shapes and sizes you have.

Tips and ideas

Can you bring your creature to life by writing a guide about it? You could make up a name for your new species, and include things like where it lives, what it eats, and fun facts about its habits. Perhaps you could use your veggie creatures to make up a story, or even a stop-motion video.

Keep safe

Cocktail sticks can be sharp, so be careful when you're using them, or ask a grown-up to snip off the sharp tips for you.

Scissors and knives are also sharp, so be very careful if you're using them. You might need a grown-up to help you with these too.

39 | Make a leaf print

Lots of trees lose their leaves in autumn. You can collect some of these fallen leaves and use them to create your own unique artwork.

You will need

- A selection of fallen leaves
- Poster paints
- A paintbrush
- Some blank paper

Gathering your leaves

Think about which leaves will work well when you use them for printing. It's nice to have a few different types and sizes.

Try to collect leaves that are dry. Wet leaves are messy, and will need to be dried out before you can use them for printing. You should be able to find some dry leaves at the base of trees and bushes, where the branches have protected them from the rain.

How to make a leaf print

1. Lay out your paper on a flat surface.

2. You might like to arrange your leaves on your paper before you start printing, or you could start with one leaf and build up your design as you go.

3. Choose a leaf, and paint the surface on one side. Holding the leaf by the end of the stem makes this easier.

4. Press the leaf carefully onto the paper, with the painted side facing down. Try to be steady here so the leaf doesn't slide around on the paper.

5. Starting at one end, slowly peel the leaf away from the paper. There should be an imprint of the leaf's pattern left behind on the paper.

6. Repeat the process of painting leaves and pressing them onto the paper to create your artwork. You could use lots of colours and different leaves, stick to one colour or shape, or experiment with coloured paper.

7. When your leaf print artwork is finished, leave it to dry somewhere flat before putting it on display.

> "Autumn is a second spring when every leaf is a flower"
> Albert Camus

Tips and ideas

Do some types of leaf work better for printing? Why do you think that is?

Can you work out which type of tree each leaf came from? A leaf identification chart, will help you do this, which you can find online.

Keep safe

When you have finished collecting your leaves, keep your hands away from your face and wash them when you get home.

Winter

The arrival of winter brings shorter days and colder weather, but there are also lots of wonderful things happening in nature at this time of year.

Many trees and plants look like they have shut down until spring, but inside they are busy working on next year's leaves and flowers. Evergreen plants take centre stage, showing off their beautiful green leaves and bright berries. Meanwhile, winter flowering plants put on a colourful display to cheer us up and give a taste of the spring that's just around the corner.

Wildlife hunkers down for winter too, and we can help our local species to thrive by providing them with food, water and shelter.

Winter also brings us the fun and excitement of Christmas, when we can use nature to create lovely home-made decorations.

It's time to wrap yourself up in warm clothes and head outdoors to enjoy frosty mornings, winter walks and sunlight through bare branches. Hopefully there'll be some snow to play in too.

Welcome to the magic of winter!

40 | Become a nature investigator

Even in winter, there's so much going on all around us in nature. It may not always be obvious though, but if you have a go at being a nature investigator, you might be surprised what you find!

For your first investigation, try using your senses to explore a fallen log.

You will need

- A camera (optional)
- A magnifying glass (optional)
- A fallen log
- Your senses!

How to investigate a fallen log

Fallen logs are sometimes called nurse logs, because they provide food and shelter for lots of wildlife, and create ideal conditions for other plants to grow.

Use your senses to explore the log. Don't worry about doing this the 'right' way, just relax and let your senses guide you. Here are some ideas to get you started.

• Close your eyes and touch the bark – what does it feel like?

• Listen – can you hear anything moving?

• Get up close and take a sniff – what can you smell?

• Look closely at your log and the area around it – what can you see? If there's a piece of loose bark, lift this up gently and take a look underneath.

Be gentle when you're investigating your log, and try not to disturb the habitat too much. If you move anything, put it back when you've finished.

Tips and ideas

You could make a nature journal of your log investigation, listing or drawing everything you find.

Come back and investigate your log again in a few weeks' time – has anything changed?

You can use the senses checklist above to investigate other items in nature. Try it out with a flower, a leaf, or a stone.

Keep safe

One sense you must not use here is your sense of taste. When you have finished investigating your log, keep your hands away from your face and wash them when you get home.

Come to the woods, for here is rest.
John Muir

41 | A cheery winter plant pot

In winter, lots of plants stop growing and producing flowers. This is called their dormant phase. It's why our gardens and parks tend to look less colourful and more bare at this time of year.

Some plants are happy to bloom in winter though, and you can grow these in a container to create a colourful display. Winter bedding plants are ideal, because they're easy to find in shops and aren't very expensive.

You will need

- A container

- Some compost

- Gardening gloves

- A hand trowel

- Winter bedding plants such as pansies, violas, primroses, heather, cyclamen and ivy

How to plant a cheery winter pot

1. Fill up your container with compost until it's almost full.

2. Remove each plant from its pot by sliding your fingers around the base of the plant, tipping the plant over, and easing the pot off. Try not to damage the roots.

114

3. Turn the plant the right way up and position it in your container.

4. Keep adding plants until your container is nice and full. You can re-arrange them if you think they might look better in different positions.

5. Once you're happy with your plants, fill in any gaps around them with more compost.

6. Finish by watering your container.

7. Try to put your container in a place where you will see it regularly, so you can enjoy the flowers as much as possible. Outside your front door or visible from your kitchen window are both great spots.

8. Check if it needs a drink every now and then by poking a finger into the compost – if it feels dry, you need to water it.

Tips and ideas
How do your senses react to your winter container – what can you see, smell and touch? How does it make you feel?

Does any wildlife visit your container to feast on the nectar and pollen, or take shelter? Perhaps you could make a chart to record your visitors.

Could you plant a cheery winter plant pot to cheer up someone you know who doesn't get outside much, or who doesn't have a garden?

Keep safe
Always wear gloves when you're gardening, and wash your hands when you've finished.

42 | Home-made bird feeders

Winter is a hard season for wild birds, because there isn't a large amount of their natural food sources around, such as insects and berries. Also, birds use a lot of energy in winter just keeping warm, so they need to eat a lot.

You can help your local wild birds by giving them some high-energy bird food to feast on. Making your own bird feeders is a fun way to do this.

You will need

• Lard, suet or solid vegetable fat

• Wild bird seed, plus optional extras of oats, breadcrumbs, sultanas, raisins, currants or unsalted peanuts

• A bowl, a spoon, paper cups, a pencil and string

> In order to see birds it is necessary to become part of the silence.
> Robert Wilson Lynd

How to make bird feeders
1. Pour your bird seed into a bowl and mix with a spoon.

2. Ask a grown-up to melt the lard, suet or solid vegetable fat in a saucepan over a low heat, then add it to your bowl. Two-thirds dry ingredients and one-third liquid works well.

3. Mix everything together, until all the dry ingredients are coated with melted fat.

4. Cut a 40 cm length of string. Use a pencil to make a small hole in the bottom of each paper cup, and thread the string through. Leave about 10 cm of string on the outside of the cup, and about 30 cm on the inside of the cup. Tie a double knot in the string on the outside, at the base of the cup.

5. Spoon your cooled bird seed mixture into the cup, packing it down tightly. Try to keep the string in the middle of the cup, and pull it tight so the end isn't covered by seed mixture.

6. Once you've filled all of your cups, put them on a plate to catch any leaks, then pop them into the fridge to set.

7. Once your mixture has solidified, cut away the paper cups and hang your bird feeder up outside.

Tips and ideas
Hang your bird feeders somewhere that is out of the reach of cats. It's nice if you can see them from your window, so think about this when you're choosing a spot.

You can use lots of different things instead of paper cups to shape your bird feeders. Large cookie cutters are perfect for making fun shapes. Lay these out on a baking tray and create a hole in the centre for the string by adding a short stick before the mixture sets. Hollowed-out orange halves and pine cones are also great options, and you don't have to remove these once your mixture has set.

Could you keep a diary of the types of birds that visit your feeders? Do particular types of bird visit at the same time each day?

Keep safe
It's really important that you don't try to handle the melted fat yourself because it can cause a nasty burn. Always ask a grown-up to help with this bit.

Don't ever eat bird seed – it's designed for birds, not humans!

43 | A wishing tree for a new year

Traditions around trees and wishing exist all over the world. In Japan there is even a festival based around wishing trees called Tanabata. People make a wish, write it on colourful strips of paper (tanzaku) and tie their wish to a bamboo tree.

During Chinese New Year celebrations people throw red ribbons into trees hoping they will stick to the branches and their wishes for a happy new year come true.

In ancient English and Welsh woodlands coins have been found pushed into tree trunks by people wishing for good health.

Why not make your own wishing tree to welcome in a new year?

You will need

- Paper (any paper will do such as old cut-up cards, envelopes)
- Twigs
- String, ribbon, or twine
- Hole punch
- Vase
- Felt tips

> We all have our own life to pursue, our own kind of dream to be weaving, and we all have the power to make wishes come true, as long as we keep believing.
> **Louisa May Alcott**

118

How to make a wishing tree

1. Collect a few twigs and arrange them in a vase or jug,

2. Cut out stars from paper. 2 triangles (one upside down) glued on top of each other works well for this or you could use a cookie cutter to draw round.

3. Decorate your stars any way you like.

4. Then gather your family around to write their wishes. Make 3 for each of you and write...

- A wish for the world
- A wish for yourselves
- A wish for someone else

5. Hang your stars on your tree to usher in the New Year.

Tips and ideas
You could make this an annual tradition and keep your wishes every year in dated envelopes to look back on

You could also make some spare stars and leave them in a bowl for visitors to write their own wishes on before hanging them on your tree.

44 | Make a bird bath

You might think that summer is the only time of year that birds struggle to find water, but actually it can be tricky for them when everything freezes in winter too.

You can help stop your local wild birds getting thirsty by putting a bird bath in your garden or outdoor space, and keeping it topped up with water. Here's a fun way to make your own bird bath.

You will need

- A shallow plant saucer or old dustbin lid
- A few bricks or paving blocks
- Some small stones or gravel

> *No matter how high a bird flies, it has to come down for water.*
> **American proverb**

How to make a bird bath

1. Start by choosing the perfect spot for your bird bath. It needs to be in an open space, so that birds will feel safe visiting it. It's also nice if there are some trees or bushes close by, because birds like to be able to quickly fly into these if they need to.

2. Lay out four bricks so that they create a square shape in the middle.

3. Place your saucer on top of the bricks, making sure that it rests on all four bricks and is nice and stable. You might have to adjust the bricks to get the best support.

4. Add some stones or gravel to the bottom of the saucer. This will give birds something to grip onto with their feet and stop them slipping when they use the bird bath.

5. Fill your bird bath with water.

6. Check it regularly and top it up if the water gets low. You might also need to remove leaves and twigs that have blown into the water.

If your bird bath freezes, you can pour in some warm water to melt the ice. Don't ever use de-icer or salt to defrost your bird bath, as these are both very harmful to birds.

Tips and ideas

Once you've made your bird bath, you can watch the birds who come for a drink. They might even put on a show for you by having a bath. You could use a bird guide book or website to help you find out more about your visitors.

Do different types of birds use your bird bath in different ways?

You could also provide food for your local wild birds to help them in winter. There's a fun activity on page 116 which shows you how to make your own bird feeders.

Keep safe

Always wash your hands after topping up your bird bath.

45 | The science of snow

Snow is amazing!

As well as being fun to play in and beautiful to look at, snow is a fantastic natural material to learn about.

Snowy facts

Snow crystals are formed in clouds when the temperature is really cold. Water vapour freezes onto a particle of dust or another solid material, creating a snow crystal. This crystal collides with other snow crystals, creating a snowflake. Each snowflake can contain as many as 200 crystals.

Every single snowflake has a geometrical shape with five points, but each one is unique – no two snowflakes are the same. Just think about that for a minute!

Snow isn't actually white. The flakes are colourless and translucent, which means light can't pass through them easily and gets reflected instead. This reflecting of light is what makes snow look white.

Snow is used by animals and humans to create shelter. This might seem odd given how cold it is, but snow traps air easily, which makes it a good insulator. Animals create snow caves to hibernate in, and humans use snow 'bricks' to make igloos. Snow can also act as an insulating layer for plants, protecting them from harsh temperatures.

> " When snow falls, nature listens.
> Antoinette Van Kleef "

Fun ideas for snow play

When it's snowing, you can catch some flakes on a dark piece of paper or cloth, and use a magnifying glass to study them. This works best if you keep your snowflakes outside, so they don't melt. Perhaps you could draw what you see?

Once the snow has settled on the ground, you can use a stick to write in it, or make shapes and patterns with cookie cutters.

Another fun activity is to 'paint' snow. To do this, fill a spray bottle with water and a few drops of food colouring, then spray the snow to build up your painting. You can experiment with different colours and different bottle nozzles to create a snowy masterpiece.

And of course, you could make a snowman, go sledging, or have a big snowball fight!

Top tips for making the perfect snowman

1. Build your snowman in a flat, shady spot.

2. Pack snow around the base of the body to provide support.

3. Flatten the top of each ball before placing the next one on top.

4. Stones, shells and bottle tops make great eyes, mouths and buttons. Sticks are great for arms, and veggies make good noses.

5. Add accessories to give your snowman character – you could try a scarf, hat, mittens, glasses, earmuffs, or even a cosy jumper!

46 | One stick, endless fun

If you find a great stick with lots of little branches, then you have found the best crafting material ever. Each of these projects was created with just one stick and in one afternoon. Which one will you try first?

Robin art
Use your stick as a tree for a fingerprint robin to rest in.

You will need

- Some red and brown paint
- A piece of paper
- A black pen
- Glue
- Part of your stick

Put a blob of red paint on your fingertip and then a blob of brown paint immediately below it. Press your fingertip down onto the middle of your piece of paper. You might need to practise a bit first to get the shape that you want. Once the paint is dry, simply draw on a beak and two legs with your black pen.

Glue a piece of your stick to the paper, so it looks like the robin is standing on a branch.

> **Creativity is... seeing something that doesn't exist already.**
> Michelle Shea

Mini camp fire

Whether to decorate your bedroom shelf or set your little minifigures around it, a tiny camp fire is perfect for winter.

You will need

- Leaves in shades of yellow, brown and orange
- Scissors
- A glue stick
- A piece of card
- A broken-up piece of stick
- A small stone

Simply cut small flame shapes out of your leaves and stick them together at the bottom onto a small strip of card.

Next, pile up your pieces of stick to look like firewood and hide the small stone behind them. Then slide your leaves in between the sticks and the stone so your flames stand up and appear to be coming out the top of the firewood (the stone should be hidden).

Clay hedgehog

Pieces of your stick would make the perfect spikes on a clay hedgehog.

You will need

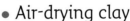

- Air-drying clay
- Broken bits of stick
- Some black paint

Simply mould your clay into a hedgehog shape with a curved back and a curved-up pointy nose. Take a little circle of clay for the end of the nose and two little dots for eyes. Add them on and paint them black with a thin paintbrush.

Next, break your stick into lots of pieces and poke them in all over your hedgehog's back to create the spikes. Leave your hedgehog to dry.

125

Christmas tree

You could decorate your stick to create the perfect Christmas tree for your bedroom!

You will need

- A stick with branches

- A vase or pot

- Some soil or compost

- Large beads in various colours

This could not be easier! Simply fill your vase with soil and stand the twig in it, then thread the beads onto the branches. You might even want to add a little tinsel!

Noughts and crosses

Create a noughts and crosses board using equal lengths of stick.

You will need

- 4 equal lengths of stick
- 4 stones
- 4 shells (or stones in a different colour)

Place two of the stick pieces down, parallel to each other and far enough apart to fit a stone or shell between them. Next, place the other two sticks over the first two, but at an angle of 90 degrees to them. You should now have a grid pattern with nine equal squares.

Choose who is going to be shells and who will be stones, then take it in turns to put them into the empty spaces. The winner is the first person who fills three squares in a line, in any direction.

Mini mandala

You can make a mini mandala or pattern with your leftover sticks.

You will need

- Bits of stick
- Some petals
- Coloured pens
- A stone

All a mandala needs is something in the centre and a circular pattern of any kind radiating out from it like the sun. This is a brilliant way to use up your leftover little bits of stick!

47 | Pine cone Christmas decorations

Christmas is a great time of year to have fun with nature crafts. Here are two simple pine cone crafts for making your own Christmas decorations.

You will need

- Pine cones
- Poster paints and paintbrush
- Some white air-drying clay
- PVA glue
- Mini pompoms
- Some string

Gathering your pine cones
Pine cones come from pine trees, which are part of the conifer tree family. Pine trees are evergreen, which means they don't shed their leaves in autumn. They do drop their pine cones, though, as these contain the seeds, and you can have fun collecting and crafting with them.

You will find pine cones lying on the ground near the base of pine trees in autumn and winter. Your local park or woodland are good places to look.

How to make a pine cone tree decoration

1. Use a paintbrush to add a dab of glue to your pine cone.

2. Push a mini pompom into the dab of glue.

3. Keep adding pompoms until your pine cone looks nicely decorated. You might like to try a variety of colour combinations on different pine cones.

4. Once the glue has dried, cut a length of string and tie it around the top of the pine cone, with the top in the middle of the string. Tie both ends of the string together to make a large loop.

5. Now you're ready to hang up your decorations!

How to make pine cone Christmas trees

1. Start by painting your pine cones. Each pine cone will become a little Christmas tree, so you might like to paint them traditional green, or use white paint to create a snowy tree, or go super-bright with neon paints.

2. If you want to add fine details to your pine cones, let the first coat of paint dry completely first.

3. You could use bright colours to create baubles, metallic paints to create tinsel, or dabs of white paint on the tips of the scales for a hint of snow.

4. When all the paint has dried, create a base for each tree. Tear off a piece of air-drying clay and roll it in your hands to make a ball. Aim for the ball to be slightly wider than the base of your pine cone.

5. Press the ball of clay onto a flat surface to create a flat base, then push the bottom of the pine cone into the middle of the ball.

6. If you've got any little plant pots, these also work well as bases. Push some clay into them, then press the pine cone into the clay to create a potted Christmas tree. You can decorate the pots with paint.

7. When the clay has dried you can use your pine cone Christmas trees to create a festive forest scene.

Tips and ideas

Pine cones contain seeds, so if you've got any spare you could have a go at planting one. Put some compost in a small plant pot and push the base of the pine cone into the soil. Water it regularly, and you might see a cute little pine tree sprout from the cone.

Another great way to use spare pine cones is to display them in a bowl. You can pop an electric tea light in the middle to give them a festive glow.

Keep safe

When you have finished collecting your pine cones, keep your hands away from your face and wash them when you get home.

48 | The great pine cone experiment

Pine cones are really smart, and this simple experiment will prove it to you.

You will need

- 2 similar-sized glasses or cups
- 2 dry and open pine cones, similar in size and shape
- Water

How to do your experiment
1. Put each pine cone into a separate glass and fill one of the glasses with water. If the pine cone in the water floats to the top, put something on top of it to weigh it down.

2. Wait for 1 hour and then pop back to see what has happened to your pine cones.

How it works
Were you surprised to see what had happened to the pine cone that had been placed in water?

Why do you think this happened?

It's because pine cones are hygroscopic, which means they can absorb moisture like rainwater.

When they get wet, a pine cone's scales close up tight to keep the seeds inside safe. When they are dry and warm, pine cones keep their scales open so their seeds can be released.

Isn't that so intelligent!

Did you know?
Did you know that pine cones can stay on a pine tree for more than 10 years before falling to the ground?

Look deep into nature, and then you will understand everything better. Albert Einstein

133

49 | A rustic star for the winter solstice

Winter solstice is an ancient holiday known for rituals and traditions that celebrate nature; it takes place on 21 December each year. It marks the shortest day of the year and the official start of winter.

It is tempting to stay inside all warm and cosy when it's wintertime but you miss the best things about winter if you do.

One lovely way to celebrate nature and welcome in winter is to hang a rustic star either from a tree in your garden or local park, or on your front door or mantel.

You can make a rustic star simply out of sticks.

134

You will need

- 5 sticks all about the same length and ½ cm or more thick (you can break them to make them the same length)

- Some string (or for a tiny one you might want to use glue)

- Ribbon or string to make a hanging loop

How to make a rustic star

1. Lay out two sticks with their ends together, to make two sides of a triangle pointing upwards.

2. Then place two more sticks forming a cross shape, with their bottom ends matching up with the bottom ends of the triangle sticks.

3. Next lay your last stick over the other ends of the crossed sticks horizontally, to complete your star.

4. Now use your string to tie the star together at the points where the sticks meet – this stops it from falling apart. You need to tie it tightly.

5. Then, loop a ribbon or piece of string through the top and tie the ends together.

6. Now it's ready to hang up.

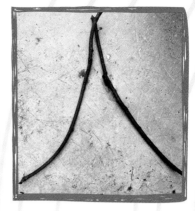

> To appreciate the beauty of a snowflake it is necessary to stand out in the cold.
> Aristotle

50 | Winter bingo

What can you spot in nature this season?

It might be cold out there, but there are still lots of amazing things to look out for and enjoy. This nature bingo is a fun puzzle to do on a wintry day.

When you spot an item, cross it off on the grid. You don't have to find everything in one go; you could come back and tick things off when you spot them over the next few weeks.

Tips and ideas

Have a think about each item on your bingo sheet. Can you work out why you were able to see it at this particular time of year?

Was it easier to spot things at a certain time of day? Why do you think that is?

136

Bingo

☐ Frozen leaf

☐ Animal tracks

☐ Frost

☐ Holly

☐ Insect

☐ Evergreen tree

☐ Flower

☐ Frozen puddle

☐ Robin

☐ Spider's web
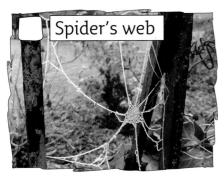

☐ Squirrel

☐ Snowman

"In all things of nature there is something of the marvellous."
Aristotle

51 | Make a winter garland

A winter garland is a simple way to bring a little bit of the outdoors into your home, and to celebrate all that nature has to offer at this time of year.

Head out for a winter walk, and collect some nature treasures along the way, then you can turn them into a rustic garland when you get home.

You will need

- A variety of nature treasures that you have found. Clusters of berries, twigs, seed pods, evergreen leaves and feathers all work really well for a winter garland.

- Some string

Gathering your nature treasures

Trees, bushes and plants are all great sources of winter nature treasures. Make sure you protect nature by only collecting things that have already fallen to the ground – don't pick things from trees and plants.

How to make a winter garland

1. Decide how long you would like your garland to be, then cut a length of string about 40 cm longer.

2. Leave about 15 cm at each end of.

3. Starting at one end, tie your nature treasures onto the string, using a simple knot each time. Space your treasures out evenly as you go.

4. Make a loop at each end of the string, and secure them in a knot close to the bottom, to create hanging loops.

5. Hang your winter garland up.

> Study nature, love nature, stay close to nature. It will never fail you.
> Frank Lloyd Wright

Tips and ideas

You could give your winter garland a lovely scent by adding dried cinnamon sticks or dried orange slices.

A winter garland looks great hanging outdoors too. If it has berries on it your local wild birds might pay it a visit.

Keep safe

When you have finished collecting your nature treasures, keep your hands away from your face and wash them when you get home.

Never put any berries or nature treasures in your mouth.

52 | Make an ice ring

An ice ring is a really fun and easy thing to make. You could display it inside or outside – the length of time it lasts will depend on where it is and how cold it is.

You will need

- A bowl that is suitable for freezing

- A cup that is smaller than your bowl (a small plastic beaker is ideal)

- Water

- Garden bits and bobs (like holly, fern, red berries)

- A freezer with room to stand your bowl up

- A plate (optional)

- A tealight or candle (optional)

How to make your ice ring
1. Fill the bowl with water and put the cup in the middle.

2. Add your garden bits and bobs to the water, and gently push them into the positions you want them to stay in.

3. Carefully place the bowl in the freezer, and leave it overnight.

4. Next morning, bring it out and let it thaw slightly so you can remove the cup. Pop it back into the freezer until you're ready to use it as a table decoration.

Question: What's an ig?
Answer: A snow house without a loo!

How to present it

You can either leave your ice creation in the bowl, or take it out and stand it on a plate. You could pop a tealight in the middle and put in on your table.

If you want to display it outside, consider using an LED tealight. If it is very cold outside, the ice ring will stay frozen for ages.

If you want to pop the ice ring out of the bowl then place the bowl in shallow warm water in your washing-up bowl until the ice starts to come loose, then gently ease it out.

Index